Making
the Grade

*An Interactive Course
in English
for Academic Purposes*

Making the Grade

An Interactive Course in English for Academic Purposes

David Wood
Carleton University

READING

LISTENING

WRITING

SPEAKING

Prentice Hall Allyn and Bacon Canada
Scarborough, Ontario

Canadian Cataloguing in Publication Data

Wood, David (David Claude), 1957–
     Making the grade : an interactive course in English
for academic purposes

ISBN 0-13-739608-2

1. English language – Textbooks for second language
learners.* I. Title.

PE1128.W66 1998   428.2'4   C97-930757-0

 © 1998 Prentice-Hall Canada Inc., Scarborough, Ontario
A Division of Simon & Schuster/A Viacom Company

Prentice-Hall, Inc., Upper Saddle River, New Jersey
Prentice-Hall International (UK) Limited, London
Prentice-Hall of Australia, Pty. Limited, Sydney
Prentice-Hall Hispanoamericana, S.A., Mexico City
Prentice-Hall of India Private Limited, New Delhi
Prentice-Hall of Japan, Inc., Tokyo
Simon & Schuster Southeast Asia Private Limited, Singapore
Editora Prentice-Hall do Brasil, Ltda., Rio de Janeiro

ISBN 0-13-739608-2

Acquisitions Editor: Dominique Roberge
Developmental Editor: Marta Tomins
Production Editor: Amber Wallace
Copy Editor: Becky Vogan
Editorial Assistant: Ivetka Vasil
Production Coordinator: Jane Schell
Permissions: Marijke Leupen
Cover Design: Alex Li
Interior Design: Arlene Edgar
Page Layout: Arlene Edgar

1 2 3 4 5   BBG   01 00 99 98 97

Printed and bound in the United States of America.

Visit the Prentice Hall Canada Web site! Send us your comments,
browse our catalogues, and more at **www.phcanada.com**. Or reach us
through e-mail at **phabinfo_pubcanada@prenhall.com**.

To my father, Claude W. Wood (1920–1995),
a leader in education.

Brief Table of
Contents

Table of Contents

3   Love: What is Love? 51

4   Cultural Shock and Adjustment: How Are We Coping? 63

Acknowledgements

The students who have inspired me and enriched the experience of materials development deserve special thanks for their key role in the development of *Making the Grade*. Many other people have also contributed to the creation of this book, which truly is a product of the influences of professional colleagues, academic mentors, and friends and family.

Professional

Thanks to my colleagues at Carleton University's School of Linguistics and Applied Language Studies. Particular gratitude must go to Ian Pringle, Director, for opportunity and leadership, and to Dr. Pat Currie for inspiration. As well, teaching colleagues who have used the materials deserve special mention: Soo Kiak Loy, Lysbeth White, Linda Librande, Petra Watzlawik-Li, Susan Lee, Geri Dumouchelle, and others. Special thanks for moral support and encouragement goes to Wendy Magahay, Christine Adam, Dr. Devon Woods, and Janna Fox.

Other professional influences whom I wish to thank are Howard Woods at Language Training Canada, Joyce White and Ina Colbran at the Ottawa Board of Education, and Bernice Klassen and Sophie Beare at Algonquin College.

Academic

Two special academic mentors whose influence has played a part in this are Mari Wesche and Sima Paribakht, at the University of Ottawa.

Personal

The people in my life who were so supportive and encouraging through the development process of *Making the Grade* deserve a round of applause. Special heartfelt thanks to the following: Jeremy Chee, Mary Grace Pooler, Beryl Wood, Deborah Wood-Salter, and Donald Wood.

Production

The team at Prentice Hall who made this all happen deserve bouquets: Dominique Roberge, Marta Tomins, and Amber Wallace. Special thanks also to a fantastic copy editor, Becky Vogan.

To the Teacher

Welcome to *Making the Grade*, a task-based, interactive, four-skills textbook in English for Academic Purposes. It is designed for learners at a TOEFL score level of 475 to 500, and should help to raise their proficiency to full entrance level at university or college in Canada.

The program is organized by thematic units chosen for their intrinsic interest. Each unit contains a series of tasks that focuses on meaning and progresses in complexity. Each unit culminates in a final project in which the learners are required to synthesize information and language from the unit in order to produce something — an essay, a presentation, a poster, an argument in a debate.

In their university studies, students are faced with massive amounts of reading, lectures on unfamiliar topics, demanding writing and speaking tasks, and discussion groups. This textbook is designed to prepare students for all of these challenges. Authentic texts in each unit focus on specific aspects of a theme, unfolding information step-by-step. A lecture adds another dimension to the information, and discussion and creative speaking activities integrate speech throughout.

The units increase in difficulty through the book, so students will be progressively challenged by the information, ideas, and language.

Step-by-step instructions on setting up the tasks, alternative activities, trouble-shooting tips, answer keys, and lecture transcripts are provided in the Instructor's Manual.

I hope that you and the learners will enjoy *Making the Grade*, and be challenged and excited by its content.

To the Learner

Organization of the Book

If you look through *Making the Grade*, you will notice that it is organized by topic. Each unit centres on one topic, and activities in the unit deal with that topic. As the unit progresses, the information and the language become more specific.

Each unit ends with a project for you to work on. The project requires that you take the information presented in the unit and put it together in a new way to show that you understand the information and the language in the activities.

Types of Activities

Making the Grade is a task-based program. The classroom activities in this book are called tasks. In each task, you are required to do something that focuses on meaning and information. Therefore, there are no grammar exercises in the book, and only a few vocabulary activities.

How are you going to learn language from this book, then? Research in language improvement shows that a task-based program is very useful, especially for educated learners who want to study as regular students in college and university. Task-based programs such as *Making the Grade* work on your natural ability to acquire language by using it.

Some tasks in the book involve reading, some involve writing, some involve listening, and some involve speaking. Many tasks require that you use all four of these language skills together to accomplish something. By doing so, you will be using and acquiring language naturally. For one reason, reality outside of the ESL class is not carefully split into four skills — all language skills are integrated. For another reason, by combining all four skills in class, you can use your stronger skills to support your weaker ones. If you are a strong speaker, for example, you can use your speech to help you improve your writing, listening, or reading.

A note about group work: most activities in *Making the Grade* require that you work with a partner or a group. This type of interaction, when you are dealing with new information, is extremely helpful. You will find that a group or partner can help you to improve your acquisition of knowledge and language. Furthermore, research shows that learners sharing information with other learners improve their spoken language naturally.

One Student's Experience

I hope you will find this program both interesting and helpful. Students who have used the activities in this book have responded enthusiastically, enjoying both the range of topics and the variety of tasks. Here is an extract from the final journal entry of Mohammed Ahmed, a student in an advanced English for Academic Purposes course of six hours per week for 12 weeks. He sums up the student view of the benefits of the approach used in *Making the Grade*.

As we enter this last week of our regular classes in this term, I can't stop myself from looking back and thinking how our ESL course was so interesting and how some of us, including me, will miss this beneficial and exciting experience.

I must admit I was a little bit sceptical (and I wasn't alone) about the style of our program and the idea of working in groups and sometimes as a whole class in ESL.

The first two to three weeks were tough because we didn't — or, I should say, I didn't — know anything about working with other individuals in an ESL class, especially in a class full of a myriad of different cultures and languages. I remember our first and second classes. Our instructor saw and detected that some of us in the class, if not most, were a little bit uncomfortable about mingling and working together, and he told us not to worry. "You will adjust," he said. "Working together in a group or class as a whole is better, more beneficial, and more exciting than working individually in an ESL program."

Boy — was he right! As the class progressed, I started to like and enjoy talking with my classmates. We started to work on group projects. Our instructor divided the class into groups that worked on topics. One particular group I was in was very energetic. We enjoyed our company, we planned outside class meetings in the university to discuss our topic, and we even exchanged telephone numbers in case someone wanted to discuss anything about our topics or our course in general.

In the class we — the whole class — worked together, often dividing long articles of our in-class work, discussing as a group, and later regrouping and joining other groups who had done similar work with some other articles or part of the same one. We discussed, took notes, and made some short presentations if our instructor said we needed to. At the end of the class, we came out well informed about the material and still enjoyed group work.

Our co-operation and group work in the class was like the countries of the world working together in areas of economic and social co-operation. Any country in the world which claims to be able to do it alone and to be self-sufficient is not telling the truth. Countries are better off if they work together and facilitate trade and social exchange, sport and education exchange among them and their citizens.

Likewise, in an ESL or other course, I believe students are better off if they co-operate, work together, and share class activities. This is what I believe and that is why, after this experience in my ESL class, I am now involved in study groups in my economics and political science classes.

1 Transportation: What's Best for Brassa?

This unit focuses on transportation. It involves reading about the history and the advantages and disadvantages of various types of transportation. It also leads to a lot of discussion as you use your background knowledge and information from reading to complete the unit's final task.

The final project is a poster presentation. You will study a country called Brassa, and try to design a transportation system suited to its needs and special situation.

You should turn to the final project description at the end of the unit regularly to see how much information and how many skills you need to help you complete it.

READING — *You will scan readings for specific information, share information learned from reading, and use reading to help you make decisions.*

LISTENING — *You will take notes while listening to a lecture.*

WRITING — *You will write short answers to the tasks presented in the unit. An optional task is to describe, in writing, the transportation system you will design for Brassa in the final project.*

SPEAKING — *You will talk about your opinions, background knowledge, and information presented in the unit. You will talk with other students to complete the final project.*

TO BEGIN, FORM A GROUP OF THREE PEOPLE AND, ON A SEPARATE PIECE OF PAPER, TAKE SOME TIME TO LIST AS MANY MEANS OF TRANSPORTATION AS YOU CAN.

Introduction to the Topic

● SCANNING FOR SPECIFICS

Scan the following text, taken from an encyclopedia of transportation, to find the information you need to answer the questions below.

1. What happened 6,000 years ago?

   _____

   _____

   _____

2. What happened with the decline of the Roman Empire?

   _____

   _____

   _____

3. Complete the following table with information about the history of sea travel to 1600.

WHO	WHEN	WHAT
Phoenicians		
	1,500 years later	
		crossed the Atlantic to America

4. What two things did the growth of sea travel bring?

   a) _____

   b) _____

5. What advantage did clippers have over earlier freighters?

_____

_____

_____

6. Which country had the first national policy of road building?

_____

7. When was the driving chain invented?

_____

8. How was steam power first used?

_____

_____

_____

9. When did steam power help create railways?

_____

_____

10. What other steam-powered machines were developed?

_____

_____

11. Did steam-powered cars have technological disadvantages?

_____

12. When was the "bicycle craze"?

_____

13. Name three important people in the early history of the automobile.

a) _____

b) _____

c) _____

14. Name three important people in the early history of flight.

a) _____

b) _____

c) _____

15. Fill in this table with statistical information about travel in various places.

	AUTOMOBILE %	BUS %	TRAIN %	AIR %
WORLD				
NORTH AMERICA				
FORMER SOVIET UNION				
WESTERN EUROPE				

READING

THE HISTORY OF TRANSPORTATION

Modern industrial society depends for its very existence on the rapid and efficient movement of people and goods. The transportation revolution which has made the development of this society possible has taken place in the span of just 150 years. The evolution of our present modes of travel has thus been rapid, but it has left vast areas still almost untouched. There are, for example, some 200 million automobiles in use throughout the world, but over 90% of them are in the countries of North America, Western Europe and Japan. There are other curious features as well. Although transportation is one of the principal technologies of our civilization, it would be interesting to speculate on the percentage of passenger-miles still traveled on foot or on the simplest of man's transportation aids, animals and bicycles. It even remains true that in parts of the world a man may be born into the stone age and progress in his lifetime through thousands of years of transportation history to pilot a supersonic airplane.

The advance of transportation before the Industrial Revolution has owed something to the life style of various cultures as well as to their level of economic development and technical capability.

The invention of the wheel some 6,000 years ago, for example, represented a notable advance, but the Incas and other American Indian civilizations managed very successfully without it.

In ancient times the Romans developed land transportation to a peak of efficiency, largely by virtue of their remarkable network of roads. But with the decline of the Empire the roads decayed and were not replaced, and for some 1,500 years advances in transportation by land were limited to marginal improvements to such features as harnessing and wagon suspensions.

At sea, however, the situation was very different. Ancient peoples made some remarkable voyages in the interests of trade and exploration. The Phoenicians are reputed to have sailed around Africa in 600 BC, while some 1,500 years later Polynesians crossed the Pacific to New Zealand, and Vikings took their long boats across the Atlantic to North America. Remarkable as they were, these voyages were limited in their implications for society and the world in general. By contrast, the great voyages of discovery of the 15th and 16th centuries, made possible by the development of more effective rigs, stronger construction and greater size, vastly extended people's horizons, their knowledge of the world, and their contact with other cultures. The growth of sea transportation brought increased and wider trade and communication, and it brought long-distance sea warfare and colonization.

Technologically this revolution in transportation by sea was complete by about 1600. Thereafter there were no significant advances in shipping for nearly 200 years, when man's impatience and competitive instincts led to the creation of the clipper ships. Sailing over twice as fast as earlier freighters, clippers transported valuable cargoes across oceans, and they carried determined prospectors to the gold rushes in California and Australia. But their day was short, because by then the modern mechanical world had arrived. Steam power had been invented, and was to bring an unprecedented revolution in transportation at sea and on land.

At first sight it seems strange that developments on land had to wait so long. Wealthy people lived in style and comfort at home; they had ingenious and delicate machinery (in clocks and watches, for example), yet they accepted appalling roads and primitive methods of travel as a matter of course, despite the fact that increases in business and trade made improved transportation highly desirable. Canals were improved and extended for carrying heavy bulk freight, and down the mines wagon-ways (simple railroads) were laid to simplify the movement of coal and ore through the mine, and to the canal. But the roads and road vehicles were in some respects worse than those of the Romans.

The problem of course was a source of motive power, and a national policy of road building. The latter was first undertaken in France, leading to an improvement in the speed and comfort of animal-powered travel, and giving an incidental stimulus to the surprisingly late development of the bicycle. The driving chain was not invented until the mid-19th century, but complex systems of gears existed much earlier and might easily have led to an effective bicycle design. It may be that those who could have afforded them would not have appreciated having to power their own conveyances.

Steam power was first employed in driving pumps. Various attempts were made to adapt the Newcomen engine for transportation on water and land, with little success as the engine was excessively heavy, bulky and inefficient. Though by the end of the 18th century the steam engine had been sufficiently improved to power boats and road vehicles, the fact aroused astonishingly little interest or enthusiasm. People were either indifferent to limitations in existing modes of travel, or they were suspicious of the new invention, or indeed hostile towards it. Fortunately there were those who were more adventurous, or had more foresight, and by the 1830s steam power had led to the creation of freight and passenger railroads. These opened up the interior of North America, accelerated the pace of industrial growth, and ultimately revolutionized society. For the first time land transportation was capable of hauling considerable loads at what were then considered shattering speeds. By the same period steamboats and ships were gaining acceptance, while steam-powered road vehicles had been convincingly demonstrated, and equally convincingly rejected by the public (and by some governments).

Steam "automobiles" of the 1840s and 1850s were heavy and clumsy, but they worked and there was no technological disadvantage in steam power. Indeed during the first decade of the 20th century steam cars were in most respects superior to their gasoline-fueled rivals. In effect the automobile had been invented, and although it would later revolutionize society it was as yet unwanted. Curiously it was the sudden development and popularity of an unpowered and previously unpopular mode of transportation that prepared society for the 20th century revolution, namely the bicycle. By the time the internal combustion engine had been developed, and Benz and Daimler had constructed the first practical gasoline-engined automobiles, the bicycle craze of the 1870s and 1880s had created both interest and demand and the automobile era could commence. Thus while earlier inventors had given up through lack of incentive, Benz, Daimler and others established the automotive industry, Henry Ford began production of the Tin Lizzy, and for the first time in the world's history there was an effective means of powered personal transportation.

The development of the automobile engine led to a further revolutionary mode of travel, powered heavier-than-air flight. Leonardo da Vinci, among others, had suggested this idea. Sir George Cayley prepared the groundwork and convincingly demonstrated the possibility, and with the new gasoline engine the Wright Brothers turned the possibility into reality. Society was intrigued by this new invention, and enjoyed spectacular barnstorming shows, even if it failed to appreciate the airplane's potential.

However, World War I served as a proving ground. By the start of World War II air transportation had grown from adventure to routine, and today is unrivaled for long distance travel. The great ocean liners have been forced to retire, and in the United States and elsewhere transcontinental trains are no longer commercially viable.

Statistics show remarkable differences in the use made of various modes of travel between one continent and another. On a world basis the percentages for automobile, bus, train, and air travel are 66.3, 16, 13.2, and 5.4 respectively. In North America the proportion of travel by automobile is over 85% (7.3% by air, 5.8% by bus, and less than 1% by train). In the former Soviet Union automobile travel accounts for only 9.4% with 44.4% by rail, 33.2% by bus, and a very high 13.1% by air. In Western Europe, where journeys are generally shorter, the proportion of travel by air is only 3.3%, whereas trains account for the high figure of 12.9%.

At sea and on railroads the emphasis now is on bulk and specialization in freight transportation, and on speed for short or medium distance passenger routes: by 150 mph (240 km/h) gas turbine or electric trains on land, and by 40 to 80 mph (64 to 128 km/h) hydrofoils and air-cushion vehicles at sea. For the future, ram wing aircraft may combine the features and advantages of 'air-cushion' vehicles and airplanes for rapid bulk transport; giant airships may carry vast loads of freight across the oceans; nuclear-powered submarines may transport bulk cargoes under the Arctic, thus dramatically shortening certain sea routes; pipelines may be more widely used to transport non-liquid bulk; and magnetic levitation and the linear induction motor may transform urban and inter-urban mass transit systems.

In the air the jet age inaugurated in the 1950s by the de Havilland Comet and the Boeing 707 has been followed by the jumbo and now the supersonic age, and hypersonic flight is on the horizon. Space travel has been successfully pioneered, and the space shuttle promises to extend its potential. However the current preoccupation in air transportation, and on the highways, is with improved safety, adaptability, economy, automation, and freedom from pollution. Indeed it is arguable that humanity's headlong enthusiasm for ever greater size and speed has reached a peak, and it is certain that the startling rate at which the speed of travel has risen cannot continue. 150 years ago a human being's highest speed was that of a galloping horse. Today it has increased by a factor of over 1,500 to some 25,000 mph (40,230 km/h). Speed, then, seems to have reached a peak, while the popularity of air travel seems to have passed its peak. The value of earnings has dropped, and unless it rises again, or unless technology can lower the cost of flying (perhaps by the retrograde step of lowering speeds), ever fewer people will be able to benefit. Technology's concern over the next decades will be to make transportation cleaner, quieter, safer, less congested and less wasteful, to the extent that serious consideration is being given to a return to sailing ships for certain types of cargo.

This volume is unique in that for the first time it draws together under one cover a wealth of information on every important facet of transportation. As an encyclopedia, it provides the reader with a complete appreciation of all the technical complexities of the field; of the many and various and often indispensable roles that transportation plays in modern society; of the inventive genius behind the evolution of land, sea and air travel.

Included in the encyclopedia are details of the inner workings of almost every conceivable type of engine, from that of the smallest motorcycle to that of the most powerful jet aircraft. There are extensive articles on every mode of travel, and on associated topics such as bridges, tunnels, highways, and navigation. And there are accounts of their historical growth and possible future developments. A large number of biographical entries describe the people associated with the milestones of transportation: the inventors, pioneers, innovators, and record breakers. Other entries cover specific ships and airplanes, and the numerous topics and concepts involved in or connected with transportation, from the smallest components to broad areas such as associated industries and subjects (e.g. petrochemicals and oceanography).

Transportation is an extremely important and wide-ranging aspect of our total inventive achievement. An encyclopedic view of the subject is therefore long overdue. The reader interested in the technology of transportation will find the facts here in readily accessible form, while those interested in one particular aspect will be able to fit this knowledge into the field of transportation in its widest sense.

The Rand McNally Encyclopedia of Transportation. © 1976 Rand McNally & Company.

● ORAL BRAINSTORMING
● CATEGORIZING

Identifying Advantages and Disadvantages

ROAD TRANSPORT

List some advantages and disadvantages of the various types of road transport vehicles.

	ADVANTAGES	DISADVANTAGES
CARS		
MOTORCYCLES		
BICYCLES		
BUSES AND COACHES		
TRUCKS AND VANS		

Sharing Information About Means of Transportation

● GETTING THE MAIN IDEA
● SUMMARIZING

MEANS OF TRANSPORT

1. In a group, discuss your ideas about the advantages and disadvantages of the following four types of transportation: road transport, rail transport, water transport, and air transport. Make notes on a separate sheet of paper.

2. Divide this reading into four parts and give one part to each of four groups.

3. Read the part assigned to you, and fill in the appropriate boxes in the table below.

4. After you have finished, form new groups containing one member from each of the original groups.

5. Tell the other group members the information you got from reading your section. Listen to the other group members report their information. Fill in the whole table as you listen.

6. Compare the notes from your preliminary discussion with those from the reading. Did you learn any new ideas from the reading?

	ADVANTAGES	DISADVANTAGES
ROAD TRANSPORT		
RAIL TRANSPORT		
WATER TRANSPORT		
AIR TRANSPORT		

A transport system may be described as a planned network of transport facilities.

A system contains four physical components:
- The Way
- Terminals
- Motive Power
- Carrying Units or Vehicles

This article will discuss all or some of these components for road transport, rail transport, water transport, and air transport.

Road Transport

The Way

Road vehicles can operate on paths or places that have had very little preparation. This flexibility is an advantage, because it means that road vehicles can go almost anywhere without expensive systems or structures. There are some disadvantages to systems that do not use paths. Passengers may not be comfortable, and speeds may be slow.

Most roads are publicly owned and operated, and this is an advantage for drivers or owners. It means that the road network is available whenever they want it, and that they do not have to finance new tracks or roads if they want to operate on a new route.

Terminals

Road transport systems have a variety of terminals. A car parked outside a front door, a van making a delivery outside a shop—these terminals are simply road spaces where vehicles can stop. Stopping on roads, however, can cause many problems in space and congestion.

Other terminals, such as large bus terminals, are more complex. Unfortunately, passengers often must wait some time at such terminals for the appropriate departure time. On the other hand, public transportation systems with fast tranfers need no particular facilities apart from a signpost and/or a very basic shelter.

Vehicles

In the right circumstances, cars offer fast, convenient, comfortable transport. However, roads have to be of good quality with light traffic, and there has to be plenty of parking space.

In fact, cars are often used for trips on very congested roads, and larger cities frequently have a problem with parking space.

Bicycles are cheap to run and buy, and use little road space. Unlike cars, bicycles do not waste fuel and resources. However, they are much slower than cars, have a limited passenger capacity, and are unsafe in accidents.

Buses can be fast and comfortable. They also use road space and fuel efficiently, and they are relatively cheap for passengers to use. However, they can be unreliable and slow when there is only a limited amount of money to maintain the system well.

Rail Transport

The Way

Railways are an excellent means of transport, but they need a well-developed and expensive system. A railway track has to be designed and built very carefully. This system of using rails gives trains the possibility of high levels of safety, speed, and efficiency.

Terminals

Railway terminals are more complex and expensive to build than terminals for road transport. Therefore, railways offer fewer terminals. Terminals must be located at the side of the rail network, and have to be easily reached by some means of road transport.

Motive Power

Rail transport is suitable for different forms of power. Electric power has big advantages for railway use, although it requires very expensive equipment. It gives fast speed and acceleration as well as low levels of pollution. Gasoline or diesel fuel offers another way of providing power. This is an effective means of power when distances are long and train frequency is low, although it causes pollution.

Carrying Units

Railway carriages and cars are expensive to build and maintain. In addition, they do not generally last very long. However, such carriages and cars have a large capacity and can carry a heavy load of passengers and goods. Unfortunately, the movement of trains can create a great deal of noise. They also cause environmental destruction of the landscape because the rails cut through forests and farmland.

Water Transport

The Way

Water transport may take place on the sea or on inland waterways such as lakes, rivers, and canals. Sea transport, in particular, can be dangerous when conditions such as climate, water depth, and narrow passages play a role. However, the sea can be an excellent means of transportation in that it is spacious and can be used free of charge. Inland waterways have certain disadvantages when the land is not flat, and also when the depth and width of the waterway are quite varied.

Terminals

Water transport systems generally use terminals called ports. A port should offer a safe place to keep a ship or boat, have sufficiently deep water, and be located in a place close to points of departure, destinations, and land transportation.

Motive Power

Water transport generally uses fuel for power, which implies a certain amount of pollution and consumption of resources. Some kinds of water transport are not self-propelled, but use other ships to push them along to their destination. In these cases, the powered "helper" ships or boats use fuel and resources, and they also pollute the air and water.

Carrying Units

Carrying units for water transport are usually ships, boats, and, for carrying products and goods, barges. Modern carrying units for water transport are usually built for a shorter life than in the past, so they become damaged due to heavy use rather quickly. However, these carrying units can often carry enormous numbers of passengers and quantities of goods.

Air Transport

The Way

Air transport uses air space, which seems to be both free and very spacious. In fact, however, air space is controlled, and many routes are very crowded and congested. Air traffic control is expensive for governments.

Terminals

Airports are one of the most difficult transport terminals to design. Issues to consider when designing airports include where to locate them, how to create take off and landing facilities, how to provide public access with a lot of parking space for cars, and the format and layout of the airport terminal building. In general, airports experience constant change and very demanding passengers. Airline services are likely to have delays, and passenger loads vary during certain seasons of the year. Many people feel that the biggest problem with air travel is on the ground, not in the air.

Carrying Units

There are many types of air transport vehicles, with airplanes being the most popular by far. Aircraft design varies with the density of traffic, the length of routes, and the airports used. Most large commercial aircraft have a fairly large passenger capacity.

Aircraft are quite harmful to the environment. They are extremely noisy, and the airports themselves are often the scene of a lot of traffic problems. In addition, aircraft use very large amounts of fuel and they produce considerable pollution.

Helicopters have many advantages compared to airplanes. They can take off and land vertically, without the need for large airfields such as those found at airports. On the other hand, like airplanes, helicopters are noisy, expensive, and difficult to maintain. Unlike airplanes, helicopters have a very limited passenger and cargo capacity.

TASK 4

Making the Best Choice

- IDENTIFYING ADVANTAGES AND DISADVANTAGES
- MAKING CHOICES

TRANSPORTATION: MEANS AND IMPROVEMENTS

Here is an advertisement for a small, open (no roof), single-passenger, three-wheeled vehicle.

1. In pairs, complete this table about the Norton 05. Be sure to list seven good points and seven bad points.

THE NORTON 05

GOOD POINTS	BAD POINTS

2. You live in a busy city. You have $3,500 to spend on transportation. Should you buy a Norton 05, a second-hand car, a motorcycle, or a bicycle? Give reasons for your decision. Try to convince another pair to agree with you.

3. In a group of four, draw an illustration of the Norton 05 on half of a large sheet of paper.

4. Now design the **Norton 06** on the other half of the large sheet. The Norton 06 is an improved version of the 05, costing $4,500. Be ready to show your design to the class and describe it.

TASK 5

- GUIDED NOTETAKING
- LISTENING FOR SOLUTIONS

Problems and Solutions

This lecture takes you to three cities. As you listen, make some notes to help you understand and remember the information. Each city has special transportation issues, and particular ways of coping with them.

Fill in the tables below.

CITY 1: BANGKOK

SPECIAL ISSUES	
WAYS OF COPING	

CITY 2: NAIROBI

SPECIAL ISSUES	
WAYS OF COPING	

CITY 3: BOMBAY

SPECIAL ISSUES	
WAYS OF COPING	

Transportation System Design

This project involves reading about a country called Brassa, and designing a transportation system suitable for it. You will use the skills and information that you have acquired from the work in this unit. Work in a team of four.

The government of Brassa has issued a call for engineering firms around the world to design a transportation system for this country. It is offering $5,000,000 to the winning firm. The firm must design **and** build the system with the money.

You are a firm of four engineers interested in the Brassa transportation contest. Look at the map and fact sheet about Brassa on the next page. What type of country is it?

1. To begin, you may wish to use some almanacs or encyclopedias to gather some statistical information about other countries, and compare this information to the data about Brassa. Then discuss the questions below, making notes in the spaces provided.

   a) What can you say about Brassa from these statistics?

   b) What special problems do you think Brassa has that might be important for your design? Think about the country's geography, economy, population, educational system, and literacy rate.

   c) How can you design your transportation system to deal with these problems?

2. On a separate sheet of paper, design a transportation system for Brassa. Draw a detailed and labelled diagram of your proposed system.

3. Display your design. Explain to the class how it works and why your team should win the contest.

4. Vote on the system that you consider the best.

Fact Sheet

People

Population: 32,657,000
Population density: 317 per square kilometre
Urban population (as a percentage of total population): 14%
Ethnic groups: Brassan 65%, Candrit 20%, Fragluk 10%
Religions: Animist, Muslim, Christian

Geography

Area: 103,147 square kilometres
Topography: mostly dense tropical forest, mountainous, many rivers and lakes; no seacoast
Climate: tropical heat, heavy rains most of the year
Capital: Brassatown

Government

Type: kingdom
Head of state: King Boola II
Head of government: King Boola II
No parliament, courts, or elections

Economy

Industries: agriculture, fishing, handicrafts
Chief crops: bananas, cotton
Minerals: unknown

Monetary unit: Boola (4,500=$1US approx.)

Health

Doctors: 68
Hospital beds: 4,500

Transport: no motor vehicles

Communications

Television sets: 1 per 89 people
Radios: 1 per 75 people
Telephones: 1 per 8000 people

Education

Literacy rate (as a percentage of total population): 13%
Compulsory years of education: none

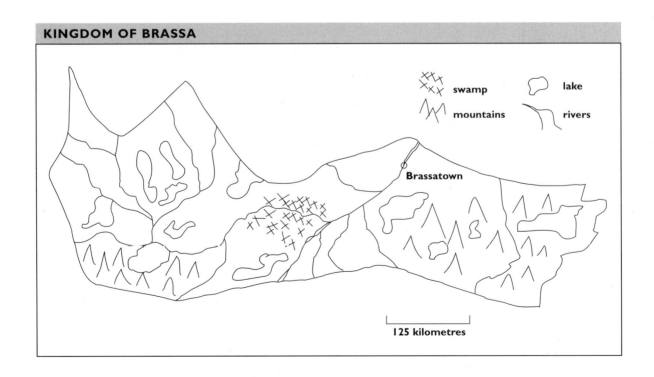

KINGDOM OF BRASSA

swamp   lake
mountains   rivers

Brassatown

125 kilometres

2 Sports: What Are the Qualities of a Successful Athlete?

This unit focuses on athletes and sports. It involves reading about athletes and the qualities that have helped them to become successful. It also gives background information about sports and athletes. The unit leads to a lot of discussion as you share stories and information from the reading.

The final project in this unit is to write a short essay about sports. You will try to organize the information from the unit in an academic way to create a convincing argument.

You should turn to the project description at the end of the unit regularly to see how much information and how many skills you need to help you complete it.

READING *You will read for information, and skim and scan academic and narrative text to get the most important information for your purposes.*

LISTENING *You will listen to a lecture about a famous Canadian athlete to find more evidence about the topic.*

WRITING *You will write short answers to the tasks presented in the unit. You will write a full, brief academic essay in a step-by-step way, collaborating with classmates.*

SPEAKING *You will discuss your opinions and information presented in the unit. You will tell each other about the rules of sport, and relate some stories about successful and famous people. You will talk and work together to write the final essay, giving advice and asking questions about other people's writing.*

TO BEGIN, TURN THE PAGE AND START THINKING ABOUT AND DISCUSSING THE TOPIC IN GENERAL.

Introduction to the Topic

- BRAINSTORMING
- DESCRIBING PROCESSES AND PEOPLE

SPORTS

Discuss the following questions, working in a group of three.

1. On a separate piece of paper, list as many sports and games as you can.

2. Does your country have a national sport? If so, what is it? Describe it. Record your points here:

3. What is the most popular sport in your country? Can you explain why it is so popular? Record your points here:

4. Who is the most popular and famous athlete in your country? Describe him or her in the space below.

TASK 2

Sharing Information About Playing Sports

● DESCRIBING PROCESSES ORALLY

SPORTS TODAY

1. Choose one of the following sports. Think about how you would explain it to someone else.

   baseball   *badminton*
   volleyball   *hockey*
   football   *tennis*

2. Form a group with other students who have chosen the same sport. Practise describing how to play it. Use the space below to make notes to help you describe the rules, the equipment, and how to win.

3. Think about how to answer questions that people may ask about the sport.

4. As a group, tell another group how to play your sport. Answer questions.

TASK 3

Inventing New Sports

● DESCRIBING PROCESSES ORALLY

SPORTS TOMORROW

1. As a group, choose one of the following "future" sports (they do not yet exist).

   highball   *seaball*
   head tennis   *football golf*
   flyball   *roller bowling*

2. Invent the equipment, rules, and scoring system for this sport. Use the space below for your notes.

3. Form a pair with someone from another group that has chosen another sport. Teach your partner your sport and learn to play your partner's sport.

4. Return to your original group and explain what you learned about your partner's sport.

TASK 4

Surveying Text

● SURVEYING A PAGE
● DEFINING

WHAT IS SPORT?

Look at the following reading, taken from an introductory textbook on sports and physical activity. Then answer the questions below.

1. What do you expect this chapter to discuss?

_____

2. How does the reading define **organized sport**?

_____

_____

3. Do Raghib Ismail and Jim Brown share a similar idea of what makes a great athlete? Answer yes or no.

_____

READING | # WHAT IS SPORT?

"To get to any professional level you have to be very disciplined. You have to have a tremendous work ethic because if you don't you won't be around very long." — *Raghib "The Rocket" Ismail, interview with the author*

"Great running is an art that is intensely personal, no two men do it quite alike. When a cat makes a beautiful run, it's poetry and jazz. That's why no coach can 'make' a great runner. Great runners are works of God." — *Jim Brown, NFL football player*

What is sport exactly? In North America most research has focused on organized sport. When the term "organized sport" is used, it refers to sport where there are formal rules and regulations, officials, a history around the sport and specific kinds of rewards in the way of trophies, titles or money.

This book is primarily concerned with organized sport. However it will also discuss informal sport, games, fitness and recreational activities. These areas are equally important because many people participate in informal sports and recreational activities. If the narrower definition is used, these other activities are excluded.

Organized Sport in Canada

The sports covered by today's media are well-known to everyone. Television newscasters and sports writers publicize those sports that are part of the sports industry and tied to national advertisers and huge sport complexes. Other events, however, are not so well known, such as the Arctic Winter Games and the Northern Games. The First Nations' and Inuit peoples' games, for example, include events that are unfamiliar to southerners.

Winners and Losers: Sport and Physical Activities in the Nineties, Carol LeClair, © 1992 Thompson Educational Publishing Inc. Used with permission.

TASK 5

Reading to Define the Topic

- DEFINING
- PREDICTING

Look at the following reading, the first part of a section called "A Definition of Sport," taken from an introductory textbook on sports and physical activity. In a limited time, look for key words and **bold** or *italic* type to help you find the information you need to answer the questions below.

1. What are three important elements of sport, based on the Middle English origins of the word?

   a) _____

   b) _____

   c) _____

2. a) Look at the definition of organized sport in the third paragraph. How many sections do you expect the rest of the chapter to have?

   _____

   _____

   _____

   b) What titles would you give those sections?

   _____

   _____

   _____

   _____

   _____

   _____

3. Define the word **competition.**

   _____

   _____

   _____

4. Name four types of competition.

   a) _____

   b) _____

   c) _____

   d) _____

The origins of this Middle English word "sport" are rooted in "to disport" meaning that the activity provided amusement, diversion and fun. Theoretically, all these elements should also be included today. Sometimes, however, these aspects are minimized.

In categorizing athletic activities, it is necessary to look at the reasons people participate at a given level and who benefits as a result of the activity. Athletic or physical activities range from being not very structured, with little competition and no direct rewards or benefits, to activities that are highly structured, very competitive and with very specific rewards. Sports sociologist Harry Edwards has classified the different aspects of physical activity using a range of factors (Edwards, 1973). Researcher Erik Allardt categorizes sport more simply by asking whether it has formalized rules, whether the emphasis is on physical strength or technique, and whether there is bodily aggression against other players (1970:27). The degree of institutionalization and the forms of organization can be significant too (Luschen, 1970b).

Organized Sport, then, is a competitive activity that uses vigorous or complex physical skills, has rules, officials and a tradition in a cultural context (Coakley, 1986). In organized sport, the athlete is motivated by either personal or public rewards.

Let us now look in more detail at the various elements of this definition.

1. Sport is a competitive activity.

The dictionary definition of competition is: "to seek or strive for the same thing as another" (Webster, 1965). Competition can take many forms. The competitor may be competing against the clock, as in downhill racing, or the athletes may be racing head to head, as in swimming. The competition can be in the form of team competition, one group against another. Competition can even take place against a record and the other person may no longer be living!

TASK 6

Reading for Specific Information

● SCANNING FOR SPECIFICS

A DEFINITION OF SPORT (Part Two)

Look at the following reading, the rest of "A Definition of Sport," taken from an introductory textbook on sports and physical activity. Then answer the questions below.

1. According to the definition in the reading, which of these activities could be considered sports? Tick the ones that are sports.

billiards	*running*
karate	*backgammon*
mah-jong	*swimming*
volleyball	*boxing*

2. What are three aspects of rule enforcement in sport?

   a) _____

   b) _____

   c) _____

3. What is meant by the "cultural context" of sport?

   _____

   _____

4. Give four examples of **public rewards** for sport.

   a) _____

   b) _____

   c) _____

   d) _____

5. Give two examples of **personal rewards** for sport.

   a) _____

   b) _____

A DEFINITION OF SPORT (Part Two)

2. Sport involves vigorous or complex physical skills.

The physical skills displayed in sport can be vigorous as in hockey or Sumo wrestling, or they can be complex as in snooker or skeet shooting. The latter two clearly are less vigorous but they do involve complex physical skills. Anyone who has ever made a bet at a pool table and tried to show off has probably found this out the hard way. Using this definition, then, neither chess nor checkers would be considered sport, but horseshoe throwing, croquet and *bacci* would be.

3. Sport has rules.

The definition we are using holds that there must be rules, but rules and regulations can be enforced in different ways (Coakley, 1986). There are three aspects of the rule enforcement in sport.

(i) *Who participates*: There are the rules and regulations that determine who can participate and how. Provincial hockey associations, for example, ensure adherence to regulations.

(ii) *Equipment*: There are controls on the technical equipment that can be used. What size balls can be used? What protective gear is essential? What should be the size of the court? Can artificial turf be used? Are aluminum bats illegal? Should video replays provide the last word for referees?

(iii) *Officiating*: Those who participate in the regulatory agencies help train young athletes and officials (such as judges, umpires and linesmen) and ensure that the rules established are in fact respected.

4. Sport has a tradition in a cultural context.

The cultural context refers to the values and the ways in which sport is played. In North America, for example, it is part of our culture that football players are male and aerobics is viewed as a woman's activity. Male ballet dancers in the past were considered effeminate. Such stereotypical views about physical activity are often widely held and become part of the cultural context of sport. Culture influences the very sport activities that a nation participates in. In Canada, hockey is viewed as the "national" sport (although it used to be lacrosse); in Italy or Brazil, soccer gets the most sports coverage and is the game most often played in the school yards; in the Dominican Republic and Japan, baseball is the dominant sport. If we look at who participates in sport and physical activities we find that culture influences participation as well.

5. Rewards and motivation in sport

The last aspect of our definition of sport refers to the question of motivation and rewards. Here there are two main elements: (i) *public rewards* and (ii) *personal rewards*.

(i) *Public rewards*: These are the direct benefits and rewards to the athlete. They include: money, incentive bonuses, medals, titles, trophies, ribbons, badges, letters, scholarships, public recognition, etc. Some people feel that professional athletes are only concerned with the financial rewards they can earn. But clearly the motivation has to come from other factors because the commitment and the training cannot be sustained merely through money. Also, in many sports there are few financial rewards available. There are not many sponsors lining up to support the biathlon or the high jump!

(ii) *Personal rewards*: These are sometimes not apparent to the outsider. They often include goals set by the athlete or individuals unknown to others. The goals of elite athletes are often in the public domain. Everyone knew that Ben Johnson and Carl Lewis were competing for the title of "the fastest man on earth." However, the man recovering from a heart attack whom we see walking quickly along the roadside might have set a goal merely to walk two kilometres in half an hour. He would certainly win no awards for that effort, but for him it is a goal he has worked long and hard to achieve.

Winners and Losers: Sport and Physical Activities in the Nineties, Carol LeClair, © 1992 Thompson Educational Publishing Inc. Used with permission.

TASK 7

Understanding the Definition of Sport

● DEFINING

PHYSICAL ACTIVITY

Look at the following reading, taken from an introductory textbook on sports and physical activity. Five terms are defined in the text. List them in the table below. Define each term in your own words, and then give one example of each.

TERM	DEFINITION	EXAMPLE

READING PHYSICAL ACTIVITY

A logical question to ask after arriving at a definition of sport is: when is a sport not a sport? What do we call those activities that meet all the criteria of the above definition—competitive, vigorous or complex physical skills, with rules, a tradition and rewards—yet have no officials? For our purposes these kinds of activities are called informal sport or recreational activities. **Recreational activities** are those activities where there are no enforced rules as to how the activity should take place. Competition and physical activity may or may not be present. The focus in on enjoyment.

Recreational activities are usually not competitive and the focus is on enjoyment and fun or play. The same physical skills are present, but the focus of the activity is different. A few examples make this point clear. An athlete may participate in a hockey league where there are rules and regulations enforced by officials with rankings and trophies at the end of the season. Here the participation is in organized sport. He or she might also play street hockey on Sunday afternoons, which would be labelled as an informal sport activity. There are rules, it is competitive and it is physical. The enforcement of the rules may vary, and the number of players most likely will be flexible. Neighbourhood participants are very clear as to what is considered to be appropriate behaviour. The focus of the game may be different, in that there are no trophies, but the physical activity is still very important. All the other aspects of defining an activity as a sport apply: competitive, specific rule expectations, tradition, etc, but the activity is not formally institutionalized.

The participants are involved with the activity for the pleasure associated with the activity in and of itself. Another factor may be the prestige associated with the activity. Admiring glances at the lines of the handmade canoe, the newly designed windsurfer, the sleek lines of the yacht, or the curves of the improved skateboard may take place. The purchases associated with these products certainly make up a recreational sporting industry, but the goals of the participants are different.

In order to clarify the different categories of sport further, we should also distinguish between competition in the context of organized sport and a sport contest. A **contest** is a competitive activity where there are no official rules and regulations established by tradition.

When Carl Lewis and Ben Johnson raced, there were regulations as to the length and surface of the track. There was sophisticated electronic equipment to measure the speed and officials to ensure that the starts were correct. This is an example of a sporting

competition. A contest is an informal competition. One person racing another to the bottom of a ski hill is a contest. "The last one down buys the coffee" is a typical example of a non-institutionalized competition. Whether the activity is downhill skiing or running, the purpose is to see who is the fastest. The events are competitive and physical and there may even be a tradition, but there are no officials or codified rules. Who has not been cheated of a win by a fellow competitor who shrugs off your anger at losing by saying "You never said we had to go down the same run"?

Another aspect of recreational activity over which there has been a great deal of discussion is the term leisure-time activities. **Leisure activity** is activity that is done outside the context of work and is fairly unstructured and not very competitive. Here activities such as playing touch football or soccer would be included. Yet we must keep in mind that a similar activity played by a professional athlete becomes a sport.

Recreation and leisure time activity vary from society to society and from economic group to economic group. A study conducted by the U.S Department of the Interior, the *1978 National Outdoor Recreation Survey*, presents a number of different categories of occupations and their relationship to leisure activities, some of which we would not call sport activities. The participation rates vary with occupation and are linked to other factors such as cost, availability and lifestyle.

Golf, for example, is much more popular with professional individuals than with service workers or labourers, obviously due to the constraints of time and money. It is interesting that 22% of post-secondary students managed to play golf at least once. This reflects the fact that such students tend to have more free time and tend to come from more affluent families.

Play and Spectacle

Playing is usually associated with children, but it does apply to adults as well. The girl hopping up and down her hopscotch diagram on the sidewalk is playing. The person constantly dunking basketballs in a net in the driveway is playing. Here there are no rules, no officials and sometimes even no goals.

Play is unstructured fun, where rules and regulations are not enforced. Usually competition is not present in any serious manner. Some psychotherapists have argued that one of the problems of contemporary living is that many adults do not know how to play. Playing is part of the joy of living, and if that enjoyment is denied an individual this will influence their whole personality.

Recreational activities, contests and playing are normally activities that take place in an informal context on a private basis. However, there is one other category that is important to consider—that is, sport as "hulk and bulk" spectacle.

Spectacle is the term used to describe physical activities where the emphasis is on entertainment and show rather than on the sporting or athletic elements. There has been a good deal of controversy over this question. Many devoted sport fans feel that their sport has been changed from a "serious" sport into entertainment. Sports about which this has been said include boxing, roller-derbies, and wrestling. Gradually, the emphasis came to be more and more on entertainment rather than on the sporting component.

Whenever professional wrestling is mentioned in a sporting context, people smile and think of Macho Man or Hulk Hogan. Wrestling is a sport that is now primarily considered to be entertainment. In fact, a large portion of the audiences at such events are often children. Although Hulk Hogan has made professional wrestling an even more popular sport, a fan who takes the outcomes seriously is ridiculed. The reason sports like wrestling and roller derbies are classified as spectacle, rather than as sport, is that the emphasis is not on the competition but rather on the entertainment and spectacle elements of the sport. The clothing, the personalities, the conflicts are all exaggerated. It is for this reason that people generally remember the personalities rather than the sporting skills involved. Often even the rules and the behaviour of the officials are part of the entertainment. While the referee is busy in one area of the ring, mayhem breaks out as a wrestler in another corner of the ring, to the roars of the crowd, is busy breaking the rules and hitting his opponent on the head. There are "scripts" to the competition, so the audience knows the "good guys" will win and the "bad guys" will lose.

In intercollegiate wrestling the focus of the sport is quite different. The athletes train, the officiating is taken very seriously and the emphasis is on the athletic skills of the participants. Theoretically, it is the same sport but in fact the focus is quite different.

Winners and Losers: Sport and Physical Activities in the Nineties, Carol LeClair, © 1992 Thompson Educational Publishing Inc. Used with permission.

TASK 8

Determining Personal Characteristics

- NARRATING
- DISCUSSING PERSONAL CHARACTERISTICS ORALLY

CHARACTERISTICS OF SUCCESSFUL PEOPLE

Do the following activities in a group of three.

1. In a limited time and on a separate sheet of paper, list as many adjectives to describe personality characteristics as you can. Use adjective forms such as "honest" or "strong."

2. Discuss your list, and tick or check the characteristics that apply most to **successful** people. Share this list with the rest of the class.

3. In your group, take turns telling a story about a successful person you know. The person could be a family member, someone you have met, or someone famous.

4. As a group, choose characteristics from your list that apply to the successful people you are talking about.

5. As a group, choose **one** of the stories that you have heard, and prepare to tell it to members of other groups. On a separate sheet of paper, write a list of several characteristics that describe the person in the story, and add a few characteristics that **do not** apply. Your list should be a mixture of true and false characteristics.

6. Form new groups containing one member from each of the original groups.

7. Take turns to tell your group's story. Hand your list of true and false characteristics to the other members of the new group. Can everyone determine which characteristics apply to the successful person in each story?

Reading About Personal Characteristics

- DETERMINING CHARACTERISTICS FROM DESCRIPTIONS
- SUMMARIZING

In order to complete the project at the end of this unit, you will need to collect information about various athletes and determine which qualities they share.

1. Half of the class will read about Peter Maher, and the other half will read about Joe Ng. With a partner who has read the same profile, fill in the appropriate boxes in the table below.

2. Work with a student who has read the other profile. Orally, help each other to fill in the appropriate boxes in the table.

Now that you have dealt with two athlete profiles, you will get information about the remaining six by both reading and discussing.

3. Divide the other six profiles equally among the members of the class. The members of each of the six groups should read and discuss their assigned profile, filling in the appropriate boxes in the table.

4. Form new groups containing one member from each of the original groups, so that you have information about all the profiles. Orally, help each other to complete the entire table.

NAME, SPORT	QUALITIES	EVIDENCE
PETER MAHER		
JOE NG		
ANNE MONTMINY		
GUIVI SISSAOURI		
LIJUAN GENG		
DAVID DEFIAGBON		
NICOLAS GILL		
BEV SMITH		

A Flabby Man's Route to the Marathon

Ten years ago, Peter Maher couldn't have run a quarter-mile, much less a marathon. He smoked two packs of cigarettes a day and weighed a hefty 116 kg. His health habits were especially unwise because they aggravated his asthma attacks. But when he took up running that year, a remarkable thing happened: he discovered endurance he never knew he had. The 32-year-old Maher, now slimmed to 69 kg, is Canada's best marathoner and a medal contender in Barcelona. In 1991 he placed fourth in the New York City marathon and set a 25-km world best in Indianapolis.

Yet an Olympic or world-championship marathon victory has proved elusive. "I will win one of these things," Maher vows. "I'm not being cocky or brash when I say this. I'm simply challenging myself, climbing my own Everest." What worries him is that Barcelona in August may be more like the Amazon, with oppressive, damp heat. Hot weather is his weak spot, he knows; he finished a disappointing 32nd in the steamy conditions of the 1987 world championships in Rome. But Maher has a strategy. Last spring he headed south to the heat of Florida and stepped up his usual training regimen from 160 to 225 km a week. If that succeeds, Maher, a booster of the benefits of running, may find his dream coming true in Barcelona. "The great beauty about this sport is that it's available to everybody," he says. Spoken like a guy who knows.

Bouncing Back Like a Champ

In 1986 Joe Ng was sitting on top of his world. The 22-year-old native of Willowdale, Canada, was the North American table-tennis singles champion, a top Canadian Summer Games hopeful, and pointed toward the culmination of a career that had begun at the age of eight on the family dining-room table. But after playing in a tournament in Indiana, he sought treatment for what he thought was a painful pinched nerve. The doctor's exam caused total shock: Ng had a tumor in his chest. "It was like someone had dropped a big concrete block on my head," he says. Ng immediately underwent surgery. As his 23rd birthday came around, Ng was bedridden and awaiting the results of blood tests to determine if the surgery had completely eliminated the malignancy. A few days later, he found that it had not; the tumor had been caused by a still present testicular cancer.

Putting his table-tennis career on hold, Ng spent a year in and out of hospitals, fighting for his life. "It was hell," he says. He was weak, his hair fell out, and he had no appetite for food. But the program of aggressive chemotherapy paid off. By 1987, with his cancer in remission, Ng was bouncing back. Recovering his sharp reflexes and lightning speed, Ng won a gold medal at the Pan Am Games. At the World Cup in 1988, he defeated the world singles champion, China's Jiang Jialiang. Now 28, Ng believes his battle with cancer made him a better player. "After going through chemo, my mental toughness was much better," he says. For one thing, it forced him to play more wisely, conserving his strength while he was still recuperating. That technique continues to serve him well. "I used to waste a lot of energy," he says. "Now I stick close to the table." Says his coach, Mariann Domonkos: "Joe can still beat anybody in the world." And return those tough shots that life serves up.

ANNE MONTMINY, Diving

Anne Montminy has a recurring nightmare. "The 10-m platform is at almost a 90° angle," she says, "and I'm trying not to slide off the end." A subconscious reference, perhaps, to lapses like the one she suffered in Barcelona at 17, when she fell apart on her last preliminary dive and finished 17th. But it's four years later, and the native of Pointe-Claire, Quebec, has changed. "I still have the dream," she says, "but I wake up wondering why I was so frightened."

In 1992 Montminy took the Canadian Olympic Association to court to win a slot at the Games; last May she finished first at the national Olympic trials in Victoria, B.C., despite a painful thumb fracture. She has developed one of the sport's most demanding dive lists, which earned her gold at the Commonwealth and Pan American games. As for Olympic pressure, "I've been there before," she says. "That's a definite strength."

GUIVI SISSAOURI, Wrestling

When Guivi Sissaouri was grow ing up in Soviet Georgia, wrestling was something of a local specialty. "There were even a couple of world champions in the same building where I lived in Tbilisi," says the stocky (57 kg) bantamweight. "I wanted to be like them."

"Gia" Sissaouri, 25, has just about reached that goal. "A lot of people at the world championships last year considered Gia the best because of his technique, the variety of his moves," says Russian-born coach Victor Zilberman, who is Canada's amateur-wrestling guru. Sissaouri started grappling at 10, and by 19 was a member of the Soviet team. When the Soviet Union crumbled in 1990, he headed for Canada and the Montreal Wrestling Club. Sissaouri earned silver at the 1995 world championships in Atlanta and gold at the 1996 Pan American championships in Cali, Colombia. But he takes nothing for granted. "If I get ahead," he says, "I will not give my opponent any chance."

LIJUAN GENG, Table Tennis

At the Mrs. Vanelli's pizza franchise in Ottawa's Bayshore Shopping Centre, Lijuan Geng, one of the half a dozen top table-tennis players in the world, pounds disks of dough in perfect anonymity. Geng is part owner of the pizzeria and an additional shop besides. She is also a devoted mom—to son James, 18 months. On top of that, as Atlanta looms, she plays her sport five hours a day. Last year she won four gold medals at the Pan American Games and finished fifth at the world championships. "I'm still not very good," she says. "But I'm going to get better." Born in China in 1963, Geng was spotted as a hot table-tennis prospect at 13. In 1985 she won two golds and a silver at the world championships with a relentlessly attacking style. By 1988 she had defected to France. Geng soon married Horatio Pintea, a Canadian player she had met years before. They spent nearly four years in Germany playing professionally, earning enough to buy the Mrs. Vanelli's franchises.

DAVID DEFIAGBON, Boxing

As a Christian boy in the mostly Muslim town of Sapele, Nigeria, David Defiagbon was bullied at school and took up boxing to defend himself. The bullying stopped, but the boxing didn't; Defiagbon found his slenderness and long arms could be an advantage. Fully 195 cm tall, he joined the Nigerian boxing team as a welterweight (67 kg), and at the 1990 Commonwealth Games in New Zealand, rained down blows on opponents from afar. Despite an ungainly style, Defiagbon won the gold medal.

Persistence pays. A chance 1989 meeting with Canada coach Taylor Gordon, whose boxing team was touring Nigeria, led to another meeting a year later in Auckland, then another and another. By the time of the Barcelona Olympics, Defiagbon "was begging and begging," recalls Wayne Gordon, Taylor's son and Defiagbon's current coach, for the chance to come to Canada. He was still a 71-kg "stick," Gordon says. The coach sent him an airline ticket, but on his way to the airport, Defiagbon was arrested by Nigerian authorities, who took a dim view of their champion's departure. He was repeatedly flogged in jail with heavy cables before bribing his way out and reaching Canada in September 1992.

No one calls Defiagbon ungainly anymore—or skinny. A solid 90 kg, he now glides fluidly, dealing out thunderous power with his right hand, rather than bouncing awkwardly around the ring. Reports Gordon: "He's knocked out a lot of people with just one punch." Defiagbon is a strong medal prospect in Atlanta, though he may need luck along with that new power and fluidity to overcome top contender Felix Savon of Cuba. Posing with his wrapping tapes above, Defiagbon exudes confidence. "I've been to the Olympics several times but this is different," he says. "This time I want to make sure I win a medal for Canada."

Nicolas Gill, Judo

When Nicolas Gill defeated favored Hirotaka Okada of Japan to clinch a bronze medal at the Barcelona Olympics, there was not a Canadian journalist in the arena. But by the time he emerged from doping control to collect his medal, he was mobbed. It was Canada's first medal of the Games, and the gritty middleweight (86 kg) judoka learned what it meant to be an instant celebrity. This time the pressure is on well before the Games start—but Gill, 24, is ready: he has collected a silver and a bronze medal at two world championships since Barcelona. "I always told myself," he says, "that in '96 I would be in my prime."

Montreal-born Gill started judo at age 6 and won the second tourney he entered. In 1990, at 17, he was selected for the Commonwealth Games in New Zealand but lost in the first round. Gill prepared for the Atlanta Games in Japan, where there are plenty of high-caliber opponents. He tore a tendon in his big toe, but two months later, he was back honing his style, which he can only describe as tenacious. "I'm not much better than lots of other judoka," he says pragmatically, "but I'm more aggressive, more determined to win."

Bev Smith, Basketball

Her teammates call her Grandma. At 36, Bev Smith has cartilage trouble in her knees and arthritis in her back. "It doesn't surprise me anymore," says the 1.85-m-tall guard, "when something new is sore." That's the pain; then there's the gain. Smith has played 18 years of international-level basketball, the most—by one year—on a team full of veterans, and the experience comes in handy. She and her cohort average more than seven years apiece in international play, and all but one play professionally in Europe.

But Smith's longevity and doggedness stand out. At 20, she started for Canada at the 1979 world championships, won a bronze medal and earned a spot on the tournament all-star team. By 1984 she was already a veteran on the squad that finished a frustrating fourth at the Los Angeles Games. Then came a long stint in the Italian pro league, and in 1993 a much heralded return to the national team. "We're a small team," Smith says, "and physically we're not the most talented. But we use our experience to win." Go, Granny, go!

A Classic Example

- LISTENING FOR EVIDENCE TO CONFIRM OR EXPAND CHARACTERISTICS

VICKI KEITH

In Task 8 you created a list of characteristics that seem to be common to successful people, and in Task 9 you studied athlete profiles and biographies.

1. Now listen to the story of the swimmer Vicki Keith. As you listen, take notes on Vicki Keith's athletic career.

2. When you have finished listening, form a group of three and discuss the characteristics of Vicki Keith that seem to have contributed to her athletic accomplishments.

3. Share your discussion results as a class.

4. In the table below, list the qualities that make Vicki Keith a successful athlete and the evidence for each quality.

QUALITIES	EVIDENCE

Essay

Write a short (one to two pages) essay on the following topic:

What are the qualities of a successful athlete?

In writing the essay, use facts about the lives of some of the athletes we have read about in class.

For each step of this process, discuss and share your ideas with a partner. Use separate sheets of paper for this activity.

1. Look at the table of athletes and their qualities that you completed in Task 9.

2. Make a list of some common or important qualities shared by the athletes.

3. Beside each item on your list, write the names of some athletes who share this quality.

4. For each athlete you have listed for each quality, make a few notes about his or her story.

5. Using your notes from steps 2, 3, and 4 above, write one short paragraph about each quality, and support your ideas with information about the athletes. Use the first sentence of each paragraph to identify the quality, and then go on to discuss the athletes who possess that quality.

6. Write a brief introductory paragraph. In it, state that there are qualities that make a successful athlete, and list those qualities.

7. Write a brief concluding paragraph. In it, restate the qualities you have discussed, and explain how you have proven their importance.

Put the essay together. Take time to revise and edit your work by discussing your essay with a partner or two. Don't forget to give your essay a title.

3 Love: What Is Love?

This unit focuses on love. It involves reading, listening, speaking, and writing about various aspects of love. It also leads to a lot of discussion as you use your background knowledge and information from reading and listening to complete the unit's final task.

The final project is a poster fair. You will create a poster illustrating some aspect of love, and will try to incorporate information and skills acquired in the unit.

You should turn to the final project description at the end of the unit regularly to see how much information and how many skills you need to help you complete it.

READING *You will read in detail, and skim and scan academic text to understand how love has been studied and analysed.*

LISTENING *You will listen to a lecture for academic information and answer a variety of questions on it within a specific time frame. As well, you will share information and stories about different aspects of the topic.*

WRITING *You will write short answers to the tasks presented in the unit, stories you have shared, and questions to be used in a survey. An optional task is to describe one of the aspects of love presented in the final poster fair.*

SPEAKING *You will talk about problems, give advice, tell stories, and discuss information presented in the unit. You will talk together to complete the final project.*

TO BEGIN, TURN THE PAGE AND READ THE INSTRUCTIONS FOR THE FIRST TASK, WHICH INVOLVES STORYTELLING.

Introducing the Topic Through Storytelling

- NARRATING
- PRESENTING ORALLY

LOVE STORIES

1. Think about a love story from your culture. Take some time to make some notes about it on a separate piece of paper. Ask the teacher for any help you may need with vocabulary, grammar, or pronunciation of new words.

2. Practise telling your story to another person in the class. Try to find someone from another culture. Now find another person and practise again. Use your discussion with these two partners to help you tell the story fully and in an understandable way.

3. Form a group of three. Take turns to tell your stories. While in the group, take notes on one of the other two stories—the one you find most interesting, or the one you understand the best.

4. Write the story that you took notes on. Show it to the person who told it. Did you get it right? If there are errors in your written version, correct them during your discussion.

Reading About Problems, Giving Advice

- READING NARRATIVE
- BRAINSTORMING
- GIVING ADVICE

ADVICE ABOUT LOVE

Read the following story and, in a group of three, take a few minutes to reach an agreement about what advice to give Frank. Share your advice with the class.

Frank is a shy 32-year-old teacher. He comes from a rural family with very strong religious beliefs. He had a sheltered childhood, and has never been sociable. He likes to read and collect stamps, and he has never had a girlfriend.

Several months ago, he met Lily, an active, energetic, outgoing woman from Montreal. The two of them have been enjoying each other's company a great deal, and they have found that they are able to overcome their differences through the strength of their mutual attraction. They even think seriously about sharing their future together. Frank has never felt such excitement about or affection for anyone, and Lily has brought a lot of joy into his life.

Frank's family members are very unhappy about his relationship with Lily, and they are asking him to break up with her. They are concerned for a number of reasons: Lily's personality is so different from Frank's, she doesn't follow any particular religious faith, she has a three-year-old daughter, and she is on welfare. As well, she is still married to the father of her daughter, although they have been separated for about a year. Finally, Lily is about five years older than Frank.

Writing and Reading About Problems, Giving Advice

- WRITING FOR HELP
- WRITING TO GIVE HELP
- FORMULATING QUESTIONS
- INTERVIEWING
- REPORT WRITING

THE LOVE DOCTOR

1. Write a letter asking for advice on a personal, love-related issue. Sign a false name such as "Heartbroken" or "Sleepless in Seattle" or "Out of Love in the City."

2. Answer the letter you receive from someone else. Give some brief advice and sign a false name such as "Love Doctor" or "Heart Mender."

3. Read the letter you have received from the advice-giver. Write another letter telling her or him more about the situation, explaining that the advice was not enough or that it was not helpful. Sign the same name that you used in step 1 above.

4. Read the letter that you have received from the person you gave advice to before. Answer this letter, expanding on your advice or giving new advice to be more helpful. Sign the same name that you used in step 2 above.

5. Read the second letter of advice. See if you can guess who the *real* writer is.

6. Go around the class and find out the types of problems that people wrote about in their letters. What are the common types of problems? List them here:

7. In a small group, prepare a short survey (four or five questions) to ask the rest of the class for their advice on how to solve the problems you identified in step 6 above. Write the questions on a separate sheet of paper, leaving plenty of space after each to record the answers.

8. Conduct your survey. **Be sure to record all the answers.**

9. Look at the types of advice that your classmates gave each other in step 2 and step 4 above. Look at the answers to your questions on the survey. What similarities and differences do you see? Write a short report about your observations.

Reading for Background Information

● READING FOR COMPLETE
UNDERSTANDING

1. Look at the title of the following newspaper article. What do you expect the article to discuss?

   _____

   _____

2. Look at the subtitle. What new information do you expect to find in the article?

   _____

   _____

3. Look at the first paragraph. What is its main idea?

   _____

   _____

4. Look at the second paragraph. What is the main point of this paragraph?

   _____

   _____

5. What change in thinking is introduced in the third paragraph?

   _____

   _____

6. Paragraphs 4, 5, and 6 describe a social fact that anthropologists are discussing. What is that fact?

   _____

   _____

7. Paragraph 7 repeats one of the ideas from paragraphs 2 and 3. What idea is that?

   _____

   _____

8. How do anthropologists define "romantic love"?

   _____

   _____

9. Why do anthropologists assume that societies in which life is hard have less romantic love?

_____

_____

_____

10. Explain the study of Jankowiak and Fischer.

_____

_____

_____

_____

11. How does Nisa explain romantic love?

_____

_____

_____

READING

LOVE CONQUERED ALL

Anthropologists are beginning to recognize that romantic love has always been around

BY DAVID GOLEMAN
The New York Times

New York

If, as Stendhal said, "Love is like a fever," then that fever infects all peoples, anthropologists say.

Some influential Western social historians have argued that romance was a product of European medieval culture that spread only recently to other cultures.

They dismissed romantic tales from other cultures as representing the behavior of just the élites. Under the sway of this view, Western anthropologists did not even look for romantic love among the peoples they studied. But they are now beginning to think that romantic love is universal and is a rogue legacy of humanity's shared evolutionary past.

The fact that it does not loom large in anthropology, they say, reflects the efforts most societies have made to quash the unruly inclination.

In many countries, they suspect, what appears to be romance newly in bloom is rather the flowering of instincts that were always there, but held in check by tradition and custom. Romantic ardor has long been at odds with social institutions that knit peoples together in an orderly fashion: romantic choices rarely match the "proper" mates a family would select. In that light, falling in love has been seen by many peoples throughout the world as a dangerous and subversive—though undeniably alluring—act, one warned against in folk tale and legend.

"For decades anthropologists and other scholars have assumed romantic love was unique to the modern West," said Leonard Plotnicav, an anthropologist at the University of Pittsburgh, and editor of the journal *Ethnology*. "Anthropologists came across it in their field work, but they rarely mentioned it because it wasn't supposed to happen."

Romantic love is a new focus for anthropologists; next month the first scientific session on the anthropology of romance will be held at the annual meeting of the American Anthropological Association in San Francisco.

By "romantic love," anthropologists mean an intense attraction and longing to be with the loved one."

"Why has something so central to our culture been so ignored by anthropology?" asked William Jankowiak, an anthropologist at the University of Nevada, who is organizing the session.

The reason, in the view of Jankowiak and others, is a scholarly bias throughout the social sciences that viewed romantic love as a luxury in human life.

For example it was assumed that in societies where life is hard romantic love has less chance to blossom, because higher economic standards and more leisure time create more opportunity for dalliance. That also contributed to the belief that romance was for the ruling class, not the peasants.

Last year Jankowiak and Edward Fischer published in *Ethnology* the first cross-cultural study, systematically comparing romantic love in many cultures.

In the survey of 166 cultures, they found what they considered clear evidence that romantic love was known in 147 of them.

Some of the evidence came from tales about lovers, or folklore that offered love potions or other advice on making someone fall in love.

Another source was accounts by informants to anthropologists. For example, Nisa, a Kung woman among the Bushmen of the Kalahari, made a clear distinction between the affection she felt for her husband, and that she felt for her lovers, which was "passionate and exciting," though fleeting.

Of these extramarital affairs, she said: "When two people come together their hearts are on fire and their passion is very great. After a while, the fire cools and that's how it stays."

In an editorial note to the cross-cultural survey of romantic love, Plotnicav wrote that, in retrospect, it was an oversight to ignore the topic in his own field work.

TASK 5

Sharing Information and Opinions from Reading About the Topic

- GETTING THE MAIN IDEA
- SUMMARIZING
- EXPRESSING OPINIONS BASED ON READING

MYTHS ABOUT LOVE

This textbook excerpt describes four myths about love.

1. Divide the four myths about love equally among class members and read them.

2. All the people reading the same myth should then join together, discuss the reading, and write some notes in the table below.

3. Now, form new groups with one person from each of the four myth groups. Help each other to complete the table below. Use your own words as much as possible.

DESCRIPTION OF MYTH	EXPLANATION OF MYTH
MYTH NO. 1	
MYTH NO. 2	
MYTH NO. 3	
MYTH NO. 4	

4. Do you agree or disagree that these are myths? Are any of them actually true? Discuss these points as a class.

Love is a highly idealized concept, and some interesting myths have been nurtured by this idealism. Accordingly, our first task is to take a realistic look at love and dispel some of these problematic notions.

Myth No. 1: When you fall in love, you'll know it. People often spend a great deal of time agonizing over whether they are experiencing true love or mere infatuation. When these people consult others, they are often told that "if it were true love, you'd know it." This statement, which is tantamount to telling the person that he or she is *not* really in love, is simply not accurate. A minority of people may recognize love clearly and quickly, but most of us have to struggle with some confusion. There is no "bolt out of the sky" that clearly marks the beginning of love. On the contrary, love usually grows gradually, and doubts are quite normal.

Myth No. 2: Love is a purely positive experience. Our idealization of love sometimes creates unrealistic expectations that love should be an exclusively enjoyable experience. In reality, love may bring great pain and very intense negative feelings. Ambivalent feelings in love are quite common. In part, this may be because we tend to expect and demand a lot from someone we love. Recent research suggests that we tend to be more critical and less accepting and tolerant of lovers and spouses, in comparison with friends (Davis, 1985). Berscheid and Walster (1978) note that psychologists are often asked "Can you love and hate someone at the same time?" This common question illustrates the dilemma experienced by many people who find that their lover may stimulate indescribable anger and irritation as well as sublime joy. The passionate quality of love is such that a lover is capable of taking us to emotional peaks in *either* direction.

Myth No. 3: True love lasts forever. Love *may* last forever, but unfortunately, you can't count on it. People perpetuate this myth in an interesting way. If they have a love relationship that eventually disintegrates, many people conclude that they were never really in love, and they relegate the dissolved relationship to the inferior status of infatuation. This disavowal of love in the previous relationship allows the person to return to the search for the one, great, idealized lover who will supposedly provide complete happiness. A more realistic view of love would be to conceive of it as a sometimes frustrating experience that *might* be encountered on several occasions in one's life. Berscheid and Walster (1978) argue that love seems to peak early and then fight a difficult battle against the erosion of time. At first, love is "blind," and we usually develop a very idealized picture of our lover. However, as time passes, the intrusion of reality often undermines this idealized view. Additionally, the high level of passion experienced early in a love relationship is difficult to maintain over time. Although Berscheid and Walster may be unduly pessimistic, it is nonetheless clear that even very authentic and passionate love may come to an unpleasant end.

Myth No. 4: Love can conquer all problems. This myth is the basis for many doomed marriages. Numerous couples, fully cognizant of certain problems in their relationships (for example, poor communication, disagreement about sex roles, lack of financial resources), forge ahead blissfully into marriage anyway, thinking "As long as we love each other, we'll be able to work it out." Authentic love certainly helps in tackling marital problems, but it is no guarantee of success. In fact, there is some provocative evidence that suggests (tentatively) that how much you *like* your lover may be more important than how much you *love* your lover. Sternberg and Grajek (1984) correlated a host of variables with a measure of the "successfulness" of romantic relationships. Surprisingly, liking of one's partner was more highly correlated (.62) with relationship success than was love of one's partner (.50). Although a small difference such as this in just one study is hardly definitive, it raises the *possibility* that liking may conquer problems more effectively than love.

Sharing Interpretations of Information

● PARAPHRASING AND SUMMARIZING

THE CAPACITY FOR LOVE

1. Assign a secret code number to each student in the class. Then read the textbook excerpt about the work of Sidney Jourard.

2. Study the list of Jourard's six factors affecting individual capacity for love. On six small pieces of paper, write each of the six factors in your own words. Do not write the name of the factor on the paper. Be sure to write your secret code number on each piece of paper.

3. Form a group with two partners and mix up your pieces of paper. Exchange your pile of papers with another group.

4. Take turns reading aloud from the pile you have. Discuss which factor you think each piece of paper is describing and reach agreement. Write the name of the factor on the piece of paper.

5. Return all papers to their writers. Have people understood your description and matched it with the appropriate factor?

6. In your group, discuss whether you think Jourard has left any factors off his list. Can you add more to the list?

READING   THE CAPACITY FOR LOVE

People vary in their capacity for experiencing and expressing love. These individual differences in the ability to give love are deeply rooted in our personality structure and therefore are greatly influenced by our upbringing.

Sidney Jourard (1974) provides an extensive discussion of the factors that appear to promote a sound capacity for love. Some of the more important factors include the following:

1. *Gratification of basic needs.* People whose basic needs have been satisfied can be more sensitive to someone else's needs. A history of nongratification will often lead one to focus exclusively on one's own needs.

2. *High frustration tolerance.* Because love sometimes requires one to put another's welfare ahead of one's own, some frustration must be inevitable. Ability to deal with this frustration is essential.

3. *Self-love.* Many theorists believe that loving oneself (having a reasonably favorable self-concept) is a precondition for loving another. People low in self-esteem tend to have excessive dependency needs and often relate to others in negative ways.

4. *Reality contact.* Effective loving requires accurate perception of the partner's moods, desires, needs, and problems.

5. *Reasonable ideals.* Unrealistic expectations of perfection in one's partner lead to disappointment and unwarranted withdrawal of love.

6. *Emancipation from one's parents.* A mature adult relationship should be governed by the needs and wishes of the partners, not their parents. Excessive devotion to parental approval often undermines one's capacity to give freely to one's partner.

TASK 7

Sharing Information from Reading About the Topic

- GETTING THE MAIN IDEA
- SUMMARIZING
- DISCUSSING OPINIONS

This textbook excerpt discusses the work of John Alan Lee.

1. Divide Lee's six basic styles of loving equally among class members. All the people studying the same style should form a group. Each group should carefully prepare to explain its assigned style as simply and clearly as possible.

2. All class members should stand up and mingle as though at a party. No notes or readings should be carried around the room. Each student should explain his or her style of loving to other students, and listen to classmates explaining theirs.

3. After each brief discussion, you may return to your seat to jot down a few notes in the appropriate boxes in the table below. Then return to the party to continue sharing your information.

4. Continue mixing and returning to your seat to jot down notes until everyone has completed all the boxes in the table.

5. Which style suits you best?

STYLE OF LOVING	DESCRIPTION

STYLES OF LOVING

In a thought-provoking analysis, a sociologist, John Alan Lee (1974), has argued that there are different varieties of love. Noting that disappointment in love is commonplace, Lee says "I think that part of the reason for this failure rate is that too often people are speaking different languages when they speak of love. The problem is not *how much* love they feel, but *which kind*. The way to have a mutually satisfying love affair is not to find a partner who loves 'in the right amount,' but one who shares the same approach to loving, the same definition of love" (p. 44).

Lee suggests that love is like color, with many varieties emerging out of the mixture of three basic emotional approaches, which he compares with the blending of the three primary colors. Using this analogy, Lee arrived at a typology of no fewer than *nine* kinds of love! Six of these (the most basic varieties) are described briefly below.

Eros. This style is dominated by a fascination with beauty. The magnetism of powerful physical attraction greatly outweighs the importance of personality or intellectual qualities. Erotic lovers are confident, secure, and rarely possessive.

Ludus. This style views love as a game. The ludic lover avoids getting too involved in an intimate relationship. The key to ludus is a casual, detached attitude, which often permits the ludic lover to enjoy juggling several relationships at once.

Storge. In this type, love "grows on you" gradually. Storge is a "slow-burning," relatively nonintense version of love. Storgic lovers prefer stability over the hectic ups and downs of passionate love.

Mania. This approach to love is characterized by feverish intensity, excessive need for attention, possessiveness, and quickly triggered jealousy. Manic lovers are consumed by passion and often feel that they are unable to control their emotions. They tend to lack confidence and often seem to fall in love with someone they don't particularly like.

Pragma. This is the rational approach to love. The emphasis is on practical compatibility in interests and attitudes. If a relationship does not appear to be working out too well, the pragmatic lover will simply move on.

Agape. This type of love is described as "deeply compassionate and utterly altruistic." The agapic lover is described as unselfish, undemanding, and giving. Lee suggests that this type of love is rare.

This taxonomy of the varieties of love is not as well grounded empirically as many social scientists would like, and Lee himself admits that it should be regarded as "preliminary" and tentative. Even if the typology does provide an accurate description of the basic kinds of love, one must recognize that love may often involve a *mixture* of several subtypes. Moreover, the question of which styles match up best for successful coalitions of love remains unresolved. Nonetheless, the analysis is provocative and illustrates the diversity and complexity of the phenomenon of love.

TASK

Learning About Attachment Theory

● LISTENING FOR COMPLETE INFORMATION

ATTACHMENT THEORY

In this task, you will listen to a lecture on attachment theory. The tape will be played only once. **You must answer the questions below while you are listening.** The questions follow the sequence of the lecture.

Do not stop to rewrite your answers during the listening. At the end of the lecture, you will have some time to go over them.

You have three minutes to read the questions below before you listen to the lecture. Check your score (out of 22 points) after discussing the answers as a class.

1. a) What seems to be the occupation of the lecturer? (1 point)

   _____

   b) How do you know? (1 point)

   _____

2. What is the third model of love focused on? (1 point)

_____

3. Match the two names below with the two roles in the development of the theory. (2 points)
   a) Mary Ainsworth   ____ originated the theory
   b) John Bowlby   ____ researched the theory

4. How does the theory explain the evolutionary value of physical closeness? (2 points)

_____

_____

5. a) What time in life is most important for an infant's psychological sense of security? (1 point)

_____

   b) Why is this time important? (2 points)

_____

_____

6. According to Ainsworth's studies, what two things do small children tend to do when separated from their mothers? (4 points)

   a) _____

   b) _____

7. Take rough notes on the three types of attachment styles found in Ainsworth's research. (6 points)

8. How is this child research related to adult romantic love? (2 points)

_____

_____

Poster Fair

1. Form a group of three or four people to work together on a poster illustrating the theme of love.

2. Review the information and ideas presented and discussed in this unit.

3. Work together to decide which aspect of love is the most suitable for you to illustrate in a poster.

   Here are some tips to help you in your poster design:

   - The theme of your poster should be instantly understood, without the viewer having to study it carefully.

   - Use a simple combination of pictures, words, and other means to communicate your idea.

   - You may cut out pictures from publications such as magazines, draw your own designs, or combine both.

   - Simple graphics such as tables, lists, and charts can help, if they are brief, easy to understand at a glance, and colourful.

   - Be creative. Use clever illustrations and surprising or interesting words.

   - Scan magazines and keep your eyes open outside of class to notice features of posters that seem useful and interesting.

4. After preparing your poster, have a **poster fair**. Groups and members of other classes can then circulate and see your work on this project. Ask people to vote at the end on the poster they find the most effective and interesting.

4 Cultural Shock and Adjustment: How Are We Coping?

This unit focuses on cultural shock (also called culture shock) and adjustment, or how people adapt step-by-step to life in a new culture. It involves reading about aspects of culture and the differences among cultures. It also gives information about the process of adjusting to a new culture, and some ideas about how to deal with the adjustment process. The unit leads to a lot of discussion as you share information about your own cultural background and information from the reading.

The final project in this unit is to conduct a survey about the topic, and then to organize both the survey results and the information from the unit to create a report.

You should turn to the project description at the end of the unit regularly to see how much information and how many skills you need to help you complete it.

READING *You will read for information, and skim and scan academic text to get the most important information for your purposes.*

LISTENING *You will listen to a description of a process in order to get more specific information about the topic.*

WRITING *You will write short answers to the tasks presented in the unit. You will write a full academic report, collaborating with classmates.*

SPEAKING *You will discuss your opinions, your own culture, and information presented in the unit. You will talk and work together to conduct a survey and write a final report.*

TO BEGIN, FORM A GROUP OF THREE AND TAKE A BLANK SHEET OF PAPER. WRITE THE WORD *CULTURE* IN THE CENTRE. BRAINSTORM AS MANY RELATED WORDS AS POSSIBLE AND WRITE THEM AROUND THE WORD IN THE CENTRE. SHARE YOUR LIST OF RELATED WORDS WITH THE CLASS.

Sharing Background Information About the Topic

HIDDEN LANGUAGES: CULTURE AND BUSINESS

This reading is designed for American students of business and human relations.

1. In a group of three, divide the six sections of the reading among you. Fill in the appropriate boxes of the table below as you read the sections assigned to you. **Do not copy from the text. Your job is to get a general understanding, not to analyse the text word by word.** (Leave the third column blank for now—you will fill it in later.)

	AMERICAN APPROACH	POSSIBLE MISUNDERSTANDINGS
TIME		
SPACE		
TOUCH		
CONTEXT		
FRIENDSHIP		
AGREEMENTS		

2. In your group, share the information that you have read, helping each other to fill in the 6 boxes. **Do not refer to the text until you have finished discussing.**

3. Now put an example from your own culture in each of the boxes in the third column. Discuss these examples in your group. How does the information differ among your group members? What are the similarities? On a separate sheet of paper, take notes on the examples provided by group members.

4. As a class, share the results of the last discussion.

5. On a separate sheet of paper, write a brief summary of the similarities and differences in culture discussed by the class.

6. Share your written summary with a classmate or two. Clear up any differences in information.

READING | HIDDEN LANGUAGES: Culture and Business

Language and religion are only two of the more obvious frames of reference in which business takes place. But basic understanding of them allows American business managers to negotiate on a roughly equal footing with their foreign associates and helps American managers of foreign workers to motivate and understand employees. There are many other languages in which people communicate, however, and knowledge of these may be more difficult to acquire. These are the unspoken, hidden languages of time, space, familiarity, agreements, touching, and friendship. These languages vary from culture to culture, are often incredibly complex, and are usually as important as the spoken language in establishing good communication and human relations abroad.

The Language of Time

The unspoken language of time appears informal, but the rules governing its interpretation are surprisingly ironclad. In the United States a delay in answering a communication can mean to the person waiting that the decision is of low priority to the other person. In Ethiopia, the time required for a decision is directly proportional to its importance: the more money involved, the longer it will take to arrive at a decision.

In the Arab world, close relatives take absolute priority; nonrelatives are kept waiting. Foreigners may be kept waiting for a long time. In the Middle East, assigning a deadline is a cultural trap, because a deadline in this part of the world is viewed as rude, pushy, and demanding.

… Europe has many hundred years of written history, and the Orient has thousands of years of recorded history. In the language of time, most cultures other than ours may seem to be tied to antiquity and the time lag that we may associate with it. The Indians of South Asia have an elastic view of time; indefiniteness does not mean they are evasive—just deliberate. The elasticity of time is the length of time it takes to accomplish a task. The less important time is and the longer it takes to accomplish the task, the greater the elasticity of time.

The Language of Space

In everyday life, the manipulation and use of space have many meanings that vary considerably among different cultures. For instance, in the American business office, space is allocated according to status. Lower-echelon workers may have a small space in the middle of a crowded room shared with other workers. The top executive usually has a private office.

Supervision and Space. In many cultures, each person's office space is determined by his or her status. The operations manager may have an area fenced in by a 4-foot barrier. If employees are deemed more important, they are given more space and their offices are walled in completely. A person from another culture may wonder how managers can supervise when they are unable to see their subordinates.

Vertical Space. In the United States the executive suites are usually on the top floor and the relative ranks of vice presidents are placed along "executive row." The top floor in Japan is frequently seen as the place for the average worker. Why should the executive spend his or her time going to the top floor? The privilege of class is for the first and second floors. Likewise, the top floor in a Japanese department store is not reserved for furniture, but the "bargain roof."

Our "Inner Circle" or Social Space. Sociologists have also found that different cultures keep different social distances—the distances between people that correspond to the degree of comfort they feel in each other's presence. The distance we keep between ourselves and others is known as our **inner circle** or our personal space. Americans normally keep a distance of about 5 to 8 feet during business conversations, but other cultures are more inclined to reduce the distance, sometimes to 3 or 4 inches.

Space speaks. When business managers arrive in a foreign country, they must try to be sensitive to what space tells them. Some useful advice to a newcomer: try to be aware of where people stand in relation to you and don't back up. This, in itself, can greatly enhance people's attitudes toward you.

The Language of Touch

We also communicate by the frequency and manner in which we touch each other, customs that differ radically from culture to culture. American men rarely go beyond a formal handshake. If they happen to be old friends, they may slap each other on the back.

The relationships between men and women in other cultures are also sensitive to touching. The ease with which American women enter into touch may be interpreted as promiscuous by some cultures; in yet other cultures, American women may be seen as cold and unfriendly. Anything in the realm of sexuality is sensitive and even dangerous for all cultures, including our own.

The Language of Context

The cultures of the world can be placed on a **language-of-context** continuum. The language of context is based on the amount of communication contained in the nonverbal context and "chit-chat" compared with the amount in the formal message. A legal contract, for instance, is supposed to be context free—all the meaning is in the words of the contract. Some cultures, like our own, are fairly low context; they tend to put more emphasis on the verbal message and less on the context. In a low-context culture you get down to business very quickly. The high-context culture requires considerably more time, simply because the people have developed a need to know more about you before a relationship can develop.

The trouble with high-context cultures is it's hard to get an American to take each step seriously and to be coached. Most Americans are too eager to buy and too reluctant to take coaching. In terms of high and low context, the United States is toward the middle of the scale. The low-context Swiss around Zurich don't even know their neighbors. The Swiss value their privacy so much that they may not develop a large circle of friends. The privacy of Swiss bank accounts is legendary.

The Language of Friendship

Many Americans have offended others by refusing, or offering to pay for, items tendered as tokens of friendship. These types of encounters abroad have made some [people from the host culture] feel that Americans approach all human relations with the cynical and cold feeling that "everything has a price." The American abroad should be careful to distinguish between friendship and business relations and to find out what gestures are significant in matters of friendship and hospitality. The offering of food, for example, is a universal gesture of friendship—to protest that one is on a diet may be interpreted as an unwillingness to "break bread together," a rejection of friendships and good relations.

The Language of Agreements

For any society to produce on a highly commercial level, a complex set of rules must be developed and widely accepted on which agreements can be reached. The language of agreements may be absolute or flexible, sophisticated or informal; in any event it must be understood clearly by both parties to the agreement. Naturally, informal, unstated rules can cause a lot of trouble for an uninformed American.

In the Arab world, a man's word is considered as binding as his legal signature (a woman may not have certain legal rights in business). To require a Moslem to sign a formal contract runs the risk of violating his sense of honor. However, since 1974 many Arabs have adopted American customs regarding contracts.

On the other hand, to a Greek, a contract may only represent a sort of way station along the route of negotiations to be modified periodically until the work is completed. If an American complains about such a procedure, the Greek may exclaim, "Take me to court." But there is no court to settle international business disputes, and mutual satisfaction is reached only through mutual respect and understanding of the various meanings of the agreement.

Benton, Douglas A. *Applied Human Relations: An Organizational Approach*, Fifth Edition © 1995. Reprinted by permission of Prentice-Hall, Inc., Upper Saddle River, NJ.

Getting Specific Information

- RELATING INFORMATION FROM READING TO PERSONAL EXPERIENCE
- GETTING THE MAIN IDEA
- SUMMARIZING
- DISCUSSING SIMILARITIES AND DIFFERENCES

CULTURAL SHOCK: AN INTRODUCTION

1. The first paragraph of this reading, taken from a textbook on human relations, discusses the typical aspects of life in which Americans feel cultural shock when abroad.

   Read the paragraph and take a few moments to list here what people from your culture miss most when abroad, in a different cultural environment:

2. Discuss your list with a partner, preferably someone from another culture. What is similar and different in your lists?

3. Read further to answer the following questions.

   a) How is cultural shock costly to business?

   _____

   _____

   _____

   _____

   b) What is the key to reducing the number of early returns by employees?

   _____

   _____

   _____

   _____

4. In a group, divide Brislin's five strategies for coping among you. Study the strategy or strategies assigned to you. Prepare to explain the strategies to group members **without referring to notes or the text.**

5. In your group, take some time to discuss what you have learned about cultural shock so far from the reading and discussion.

Cultural shock (commonly called culture shock) is the trauma you experience when you move into a culture different from your home culture. Cultural shock is basically a communication problem that involves the frustrations that accompany a lack of understanding of the verbal and nonverbal communication of the host culture and its customs and value systems. Frustrations may include lack of food, unacceptable standards of cleanliness, different bathroom facilities, and fear for personal safety. In a survey of 188 students from two mid-South universities who had traveled or lived abroad, the greatest degree of cultural shock was reported in the areas of lack of modern conveniences and standards of cleanliness. Other areas in which cultural shock showed statistical significance included attitudes toward women, nonverbal communication, clothing/business dress, family and marriage practices, housing, climate, educational system, financial problems, and values and ethical standards (Chaney & Martin, 1993). The absence of conveniences taken for granted in the United States, such as telephones that work, running water available 24 hours a day, or buses that run on time, is an additional source of frustration. People with strong religious ties may feel spiritually adrift without a church of their faith. Without the bounty of U.S. shopping malls, supermarkets, and multiple television sets, depression may result. In addition to depression, people who experience cultural shock can become homesick, eat or drink compulsively, and even develop physical ailments.

Cultural shock has received increased attention by researchers only in the past two decades. However, Jack London, in his story "In a Far Country" published in 1900, stressed that a visitor to another culture should be prepared to acquire new customs and abandon old ideals. He suggested that sojourners should find pleasure in the unfamiliar because those who could not fit into the new culture would either return home or "die" of both psychological and physical ailments. London's advice is still sound almost a hundred years later (Lewis & Jungman, 1986).

Cultural shock can be costly to a firm, since it often results in the premature return of U.S. people working overseas. Ferraro (1990) quotes research that shows employees sent to work in foreign countries fail not because they lack technical or professional competence but because of their inability to understand and adapt to another culture's way of life. Estimates on early return of U.S. expatriate managers range from 45 to 85 percent (Ferraro, 1990). When companies implement measures to combat cultural shock, such as conducting training programs for sojourners (people who visit or reside temporarily in another country), the early return rate drops to less than 2 percent.

Some companies have used short-term stays of two to three months to determine the employee's potential for tolerating the culture. Sometimes these short-term projects are designed to prepare the person for a longer stay later. On other occasions, these brief trips are simply ways to utilize the talents of technical professionals who would be unwilling to go in the first place if it meant disrupting the professional advancement of a career-oriented spouse. Short trips are also cost effective, as the need to move the family is reduced or eliminated. While the degree and type of cultural shock experienced by people who travel to another country for a short stay may be similar to the shock experienced by those who plan an extended visit, the strategies for coping during the short-term visit may differ. Brislin (1981) identifies five strategies used for coping with the new culture during short visits:

1. One strategy is *nonacceptance* of the host culture; the traveler simply behaves as he or she would in the home culture. No effort is made to learn the language or the customs of the host culture.

2. A second strategy is known as *substitution*. The traveler learns the appropriate responses or behaviors in the host culture and substitutes these responses or behaviors for the ones he or she would ordinarily use in the home culture.

3. A third strategy is known as *addition*. The person adds the behavior of the host culture when in the presence of the nationals but maintains the home culture behavior with others of the same culture.

4. A fourth strategy is known as *synthesis*. This strategy integrates or combines elements of the two cultures, such as combining the dress of the United States and the Philippines.

5. The final strategy is referred to as *resynthesis*, the integration of ideas not found in either culture. An example of this strategy would be a U.S. traveler to China who chooses to eat neither American nor Chinese food, but prefers Italian food.

TASK 3

Listening to Get More Specific Information

- PREDICTING USING PERSONAL EXPERIENCE
- LISTENING FOR THE STEPS IN A PROCESS
- SUMMARIZING

1. Before listening to the lecture on cultural shock, take a few minutes to think about the following questions.

   When you have visited or lived in a foreign culture, have you ever

   - worried about the food?
   - found the local people unfriendly and unsympathetic?
   - preferred the company of people from your home culture?
   - felt homesick?
   - made jokes about the host culture?

2. Now, as you listen, take notes by filling in the table below.

STAGE OF CULTURAL SHOCK	CHARACTERISTICS

3. Compare your notes with those of a partner.

TASK 4

Reading to Confirm Information

- SKIMMMING TO CONFIRM INFORMATION FROM LISTENING

1. Read the following academic text quickly to check the notes you made when you listened to the lecture in Task 3.

2. With a partner, discuss the information you have gained by reading and listening. Does the reading give you more to add to your notes?

3. Use the space below to make full notes on the stages of cultural shock **without referring back to the notes you made in Task 3 or to the reading.**

4. Return to the notes you made in Task 3 and the reading. Refer to the reading to add to or change your notes.

READING STAGES OF CULTURAL SHOCK

Cultural shock generally goes through five stages: excitement or initial euphoria, crisis or disenchantment, adjustment, acceptance, and reentry.

The first stage is excitement and fascination with the new culture, which can last for only a few days or for several months. During this time, everything is new and different; you are fascinated with the food and the people. Sometimes this stage is referred to as the "honeymoon" stage during which your enthusiasm for the new culture causes you to overlook minor problems, such as having to drink bottled water and the absence of central heating or air conditioning.

During the second stage, the crisis or disenchantment period, the "honeymoon" is over; your excitement has turned to disappointment as you encounter more and more differences between your own culture and the new culture. Problems with transportation, unfamiliar foods, and people who do not speak English now seem overwhelming. The practice of bargaining over the purchase price of everything that you originally found amusing is now a constant source of irritation. People in this stage often cope with the situation by making disparaging remarks about the culture; it is sometimes referred to as the "fight back" technique. Others deal with this stage by leaving, either physically or psychologically. Those who remain may withdraw from people in the culture, refuse to learn the language, and develop coping behaviors of excessive drinking or drug use. Some individuals actually deny differences and will speak in glowing terms of the new culture.

In the third stage, the adjustment phase, you begin to accept the new culture. You try new foods and make adjustments in behavior to accommodate the shopping lines and the long waits for public transportation. You begin to see the humor in situations and realize that a change in attitude toward the host culture will make the stay abroad more rewarding.

In the fourth phase, the acceptance or adaptation phase, you feel at home in the new culture, become involved in activities of the culture, cultivate friendships among the nationals, and feel comfortable in social situations with people from the host culture. You learn the language and may adopt the new culture's style of doing things. You even learn to enjoy some customs, such as afternoon tea and the midday siesta, that you will miss when you return to the home country.

The final phase is reentry shock, which can be almost as traumatic as the initial adjustment to a new culture, particularly after an extended stay abroad. Reentry shock is experienced upon returning to the home country and may follow the stages identified earlier: initial euphoria, crisis or disenchantment, adjustment, and acceptance or adaptation. You would at first be happy to be back in your own country, then become disenchanted as you realize that your friends are not really interested in hearing about your experiences abroad, your standard of living goes down, and you are unable to use such skills as a foreign language or bargaining in the market. You then move into the adjustment stage as you become familiar with new technology and view with appreciation such things as the abundance and variety of foods and clothing and the improved standards of more cleanliness. You finally move into the acceptance stage when you feel comfortable with the mores in the home culture and find yourself returning to many of your earlier views and behaviors.

Although reentry shock typically occurs for a shorter period of time than the first four stages of cultural shock, expatriates who have made a good adjustment to the host culture may go through a rather long period of adjustment, lasting six months or more, when they are confronted with the changes that have taken place in their absence. Some of these changes are work related; expatriates may feel "demoted" when they return to middle-management positions without the bonuses, perks, and professional contacts they enjoyed abroad. In other situations, changes have taken place in the home country,

including in politics and styles of clothing, that require readjustment. In research conducted by Chaney and Martin (1993), the four areas in which reentry shock was experienced by college students who had traveled abroad that were statistically significant were readjusting to lifestyle, change in social life, change in standard of living, and reestablishing friendships.

Some reentry problems are personal in nature. Many repatriates have changed; they have acquired a broadened view of the world and have undergone changes in values and attitudes. Personal problems may include unsuccessful attempts to renew personal and professional relationships as the realization sets in that their former friends do not share their enthusiasm for their overseas experiences and accomplishments. They must then make new friends who share this common experience. Children of expatriates encounter similar readjustment problems as their former friends have made new ones and they find that the education they received abroad is sufficiently different to cause problems when returning to schools in the United States.

Since reentry shock is a natural part of cultural shock, multinational corporations must provide training for expatriates to assure that the transition to the home culture is a positive experience. In the absence of such training, you can do much to counteract reentry shock by sharing your feelings (not your experiences) with sympathetic family members and friends, particularly those who have lived abroad. Correspond regularly with members of the home culture; ask questions concerning changes that are taking place. Subscribe to the home newspaper to stay abreast of current happenings. Keep in touch with professional organizations and other groups with which you may want to affiliate. Many repatriates have found that maintaining ties with the home culture cushions the shock associated with reentry (Dodd, 1987; Dodd & Montalvo, 1987; Khols, 1984; Klopf, 1991).

Intercultural Business Communication by Chaney/Martin, © 1995. Reprinted by permission of Prentice-Hall, Inc., Upper Saddle River, NJ.

TASK 5

Applying the Information to Cases

● RELATING READ INFORMATION TO SPECIFIC EXAMPLES

APPLYING THE STAGES

1. For each brief anecdote below, identify which stage of cultural shock is represented. Be prepared to explain your answer.

   a) After having been abroad for six years, John was very critical of the manners of people in his hometown.

   _____

   _____

b) Most Saturdays, Maria stayed in her apartment and watched video movies from home, dreaming of the day she could go back.

_____

_____

c) Min and Jeong spent a lot of time feeling disgusted with the behaviour of the people on the bus and comparing it unfavourably to that of people back home.

_____

_____

d) Sam couldn't believe his good luck. At last, the dream of living here had come true!

_____

_____

e) Rashid resolved to try very hard to fit in with his new friends, and to get closer to them. After all, he had wasted enough time here.

_____

_____

f) Eriko longed to go back there; she just didn't seem to fit in at home anymore. She had changed.

_____

_____

g) Mei Ling found it difficult but rewarding to try to learn some of the language and talk to the people. Making an effort at last, she felt hope for a change.

_____ acceptance _____

_____

h) Karen just couldn't wait to send pictures home to prove that she was really living in this fascinating place.

_____

_____

2. Share your answers in a small group. Explain the reasons for your choices. Do you all agree?

Cultural Shock Research

With a partner, prepare a research report on cultural shock and adjustment by following the steps below.

1. Referring to the five stages of cultural shock, prepare a series of interview questions to use in a survey about cultural shock and adjustment. Think about what questions you need to ask people to get information about their stage of cultural adjustment.

    Create questions that will give you information you can easily tabulate or record to get numbers. The most useful kinds for this survey are closed questions, Likert Scale questions, and multiple choice questions.

    - A **closed question** is a question that asks for a yes, no, or one-word answer.
      Example: Are you glad you came here?   yes____   no____

    - A **Likert Scale** (from 1 to 5) is a type of survey question that provides easily tabulated results.
      Example: Rate your comfort level in talking to local people.

      1   (very uncomfortable)
      2   (somewhat uncomfortable)
      3   (neither comfortable nor uncomfortable)
      4   (somewhat comfortable)
      5   (very comfortable)

    - A **multiple choice question** can also be useful. For your purposes, you could make each possible response correspond to a stage of cultural shock.
      Example: On Saturday night, I usually like to

      a) go sightseeing (first stage)
      b) stay in with friends from my own culture (second stage)
      c) try to contact local culture (third stage)
      d) get together with local people (fourth stage)

    Write the questions on a separate sheet of paper, leaving plenty of space after each to record the answers.

2. Test your questions out on classmates to be sure your survey will provide you with the information you need.

3. Conduct your survey. **Be sure to record all the answers.**

4. List your results on a separate sheet of paper.

5. Write a report on your research. Divide it into four sections: introduction, method, results, and discussion.

    - For the **introduction**, give background information about the stages of cultural shock and explain what you were trying to find out in this survey.

- For the **method** section, describe the population (the people you surveyed) in terms of gender, culture, and other relevant characteristics. How long have they been here? What questions did you ask them? List the questions and explain the reason for asking each one.

- For the **results** section, show the statistical results of your survey. Provide tables or charts.

- For the **discussion** section, explain what the results mean and relate them to the background information and purpose that you described in the introduction. Was your survey successful? What do the results tell us?

5 Family: How Varied Are We?

This unit focuses on families around the world and changes in the Canadian family. It involves reading about family structures and the variety and change they show. It also gives background information about families, taken from anthropology and sociology textbooks. The unit leads to a lot of discussion as you share opinions and information from the reading.

The final project in this unit is to participate in a formal in-class debate about one aspect of the topic. To prepare, you will try to organize the information from the unit in an academic way to create convincing oral arguments.

You should turn to the project description at the end of the unit regularly to see how much information and how many skills you need to help you complete it.

READING *You will read for information, and skim and scan academic and journalistic text to get the most important information for your purposes.*

LISTENING *You will listen to information presented in chronological order.*

WRITING *You will write short answers to tasks presented in the unit, including brief information summaries. There is no large written assignment in this unit.*

SPEAKING *You will discuss your opinions and information presented in the unit. You will tell each other about your own families, and relate your lives to the information about family change and variety. You will talk and work together to prepare the final debate, giving opinions.*

TO BEGIN, TURN THE PAGE AND START THINKING ABOUT AND DISCUSSING THE TOPIC IN GENERAL.

● SHARING PERSONAL
INFORMATION

Introduction to the Topic

FAMILY LIFE

1. Complete the table below with information about your family.

ACTIVITY	PERSON RESPONSIBLE
SHOPPING FOR FOOD	
COOKING	
CLEANING	
GARDENING	
MAKING REPAIRS	
DECORATING	
LOOKING AFTER MONEY	
LOOKING AFTER CHILDREN	

2. How did other people in class complete the table? Find out.

3. In a group of four, exchange information about your families. Complete the chart below while you are talking.

	FAMILY 1	FAMILY 2	FAMILY 3	FAMILY 4
HOW MANY MEMBERS?				
DO THEY LIVE IN THE SAME TOWN OR HOUSE?				
WHEN DO THEY MEET?				
WHERE DO THEY MEET?				
OTHER INFORMATION				

4. What are the similarities and differences among your group's families? Report your observations to the rest of the class.

5. Tick the statement below that is a good summary of the class discussion.

   a) Family life is very similar wherever you are.

   b) Family life varies greatly.

Reading for Background Information

● READING DEFINITIONS

Scan this academic text to locate the important terms and definitions. Use the headings and words in **bold** type to guide you.

1. How does this text define **family**?

   _____

   _____

2. What are the two major types of family **composition**? Define them here in your own words:

   a) _____

   _____

   b) _____

   _____

3. What are the three types of **descent** described in the text? Define them here in your own words:

   a) _____

   _____

   b) _____

   _____

   c) _____

   _____

4. What are the three types of **residence** situation discussed in the text? Define them here in your own words:

   a) _____

   _____

   b) _____

   _____

   c) _____

   _____

5. What are the three types of **authority** discussed in the text? Define them here in your own words:

   a) _____

   _____

   b) _____

   _____

c) _____

_____

6. How does this text define **marriage**?

_____

_____

_____

_____

7. What is **endogamy**?

_____

_____

_____

8. What is **exogamy**?

_____

_____

_____

9. What are the four types of **marriage** discussed in the text? Define them here in your own words:

a) _____

_____

b) _____

_____

c) _____

_____

d) _____

_____

10. Which of the four types of marriage is the most popular?

_____

11. What is one more type of marriage discussed at the end of the text?

_____

12. On a separate sheet of paper, using the terms from the text, write a description of your family and your society. Share your description with a partner or two.

What is the family? Although we all use the term and doubtless have a notion of what we mean by it, the "family" is exceedingly difficult to define. When we set about separating families from nonfamilies, we encounter all sorts of problems (Stephens, 1963). Many of us think of the family as a social unit consisting of a married couple and their children—Mom, Dad, and the kids. But as we will see in the course of the chapter, this definition is too limited. In many societies it is the kin group, and not a married couple and their children, that is the basic family unit. Sociologists have traditionally viewed the **family** as a social group whose members are related by ancestry, marriage, or adoption and who live together, cooperate economically, and care for the young (Murdock, 1949). But those who are unhappy with this definition argue that psychological bonds are what families are all about. Defined in this fashion, long-term relationships, heterosexual or homosexual, should be considered families. Clearly, defining the family is not simply an academic exercise: How we define it determines the kinds of intimate groups we consider normal and the kinds we consider deviant, and what rights and obligations we recognize as legally and socially binding (Skolnick, 1981).

Forms of the Family

The family is a unique institution. In no sphere of social life are the differences in human societies more evident and striking than in kin and marriage patterns. Throughout the world there are many arrangements for regulating mating and reproduction, caring for and bringing up children, and meeting personal needs. Let us begin our discussion by considering a number of these differences.

Composition   Every society has a family system, although not every society has organized and relatively independent religious, economic, political, educational, and medical institutions. Social relationships between adult males and females can be organized within families by emphasizing either spouse or kin relationships. In the **nuclear family** arrangement, spouses and their offspring constitute the core relationship; blood relatives are functionally marginal. In contrast, in the **extended family** arrangement, *kin*—individuals related by common ancestry—provide the core relationship; spouses are functionally marginal. The nuclear family pattern is the preferred arrangement for most Americans. In the course of their lives, Americans typically are members of two nuclear families. First, a person belongs to a nuclear family that consists of oneself and one's father, mother, and siblings, what sociologists

call the **family of orientation**. Second, since over 90 percent of Americans marry at least once, the vast majority of people are members of a nuclear family that consists of themselves and a spouse and children, what sociologists call the **family of procreation**.

Extended families are found throughout the world. In one case, that of the Nayar—a warrior caste group in pre-British southwestern India—spouse ties were virtually absent (Gough, 1959, 1965; Dumont, 1970; Fuller, 1976). About the time of puberty, a Nayar woman took a ritual husband chosen for her by a neighborhood assembly. The union was recognized in a ceremony during which the husband tied a gold ornament around the neck of his bride. In the marriage ritual, the man acted as a representative of all the men of his group, an act that accorded them sexual rights with the woman. Without this ritual, no offspring could be considered legitimate. After three days, the woman was ritually separated from her "husband" and was then free to take on a series of "visiting husbands" or "lovers." Although a woman's lovers gave her regular gifts on prescribed occasions, they did not provide her with support. When a woman had a child, one of the men—not necessarily the biological father—paid a fee to the midwife. However, the man assumed no economic, social, legal, or ritual rights or obligations toward the child: It was the *mother's* blood relatives who took responsibility for the child.

For some time, sociologists assumed that industrialization undercut extended family patterns while fostering nuclear family arrangements (Goode, 1963). For one thing, industrialism requires that people move about in search of new job and professional opportunities, weakening kin obligations that depend on frequent and intimate interaction. For another, industrialism substitutes nonkin agencies for kin groups in handling such common problems as police protection, education, military defense, and money lending. Now sociologists have taken a new look and have found that industrialization and extended family arrangements are not necessarily incompatible (Laslett, 1974, 1976; Quadagno, 1982; Cherlin, 1983). Although industrializing peoples make new demands on kin, industrialization also makes it possible to respond to family claims with new resources. For instance, when the Tonga of Malawi went off to work in the mines of Zimbabwe and South Africa, they did not take their wives and children with them. The men relied on their kin to look after their wives and children, while they sent home as much of their wages as they could. The men continued to exert their claims to status and land in the village and took part in village politics (Goldthorpe, 1984). Similarly, when Tamara K. Hareven (1982) examined family life in a textile community of New Hampshire in the nineteenth century, she discovered that industrialism had promoted kin ties. Not only did different generations often reside in the same household, they provided a good deal of assistance to one another.

Descent Societies trace descent and pass property on from one generation to the next in one of three ways. Under a **patrilineal** arrangement, a people reckon descent and transmit property through the line of the father. Under the **matrilineal** arrangement, descent and inheritance take place through the mother's side of the family. The Nayar, for example, were a matrilineal people. A child owed allegiance to the mother's brother, and not the father. Property and position passed from maternal uncle to nephew. Under the **bilineal** arrangement, both sides of an individual's family are equally important. Americans are typically bilineal, reckoning descent through both father and mother (however, the surname is transmitted in a patrilineal manner).

Kin, then, are people who act like kin—who relate to us in certain ways and expect to be treated in certain ways—as well as people who are biologically related to us. For instance, we typically use the terms "aunt" and "uncle" for people who are married to the sisters and brothers of our mother and father, even though such relationships lack a biological reference. We call them Aunt Bee or Uncle Ed because of social definitions. And we behave toward them, and they toward us, much as if they were biologically our aunts and uncles (Cole, 1982).

Residence Societies differ in the location where a couple takes up residence after marriage. In the case of **patrilocal** residence, the bride and groom live in the household or community of the husband's family. The opposite pattern prevails in **matrilocal** residence. For example, among the Hopi, a Southwest Pueblo people, upon marriage the husband moves into the dwelling of his wife's family, and it is here that he eats and sleeps. In the mainstream American culture, newlyweds tend to follow **neolocal** patterns in which they set up a new place of residence independent of parents or other relatives.

Authority Although the authority men and women exercise in family decision making is influenced by their personalities, societies nonetheless dictate who is expected to be the dominant figure. Under **patriarchal** arrangements, it is usually the eldest male or the husband who fills this role. The ancient Hebrews, Greeks, and Romans and the nineteenth-century Chinese and Japanese provide examples. Logically, the construction of a **matriarchal** family type is very simple and would involve the vesting of power in women. Yet true matriarchies are rare, and

considerable controversy exists as to whether the balance of power actually rests with the wife in any known society (Stephens, 1963). Although matriarchies may not be the preferred arrangement in most societies, they often arise through default upon the death or desertion of the husband. Moreover, in some societies cultural norms provide that husband and wife each has spheres of authority. In a third type of family, the **equalitarian** arrangement, power and authority are equally distributed between the husband and wife. This pattern has been on the increase in recent years in the United States, where marriage is changing from a one-vote system in which men make the decisions to a system in which the couple sort out choices jointly.

Forms of Marriage

The fact that the parties to a marriage must be members of two different kin groups has crucial implications for the structure of the family. Indeed, the continuity, and therefore the long-term welfare, of any kin group depends on obtaining spouses for the unmarried members of the group from other groups. A kin group also has a stake in retaining some measure of control over at least a portion of its members after they marry (Lee, 1977). Accordingly, we need to take a closer look at mating arrangements, particularly **marriage**, a socially approved sexual union between two or more individuals that is undertaken with some idea of permanence.

Exogamy and endogamy All societies regulate the pool of eligibles from which individuals are expected to select a mate. A child's kin generally have more in mind than simply getting a child married. They want the child married to the *right* spouse, especially where marriage has consequences for the kin group. Two types of marital regulations define the "right" spouse: endogamy and exogamy. **Endogamy** is the requirement that marriage occur within a group. People must marry within their class, caste, race, ethnic group, or religion. **Exogamy** is the requirement that marriage occur outside a group. People must marry outside their kin group, be it their immediate nuclear family, clan, or tribe.

Regulations relating to exogamy are based primarily on kinship and usually entail **incest taboos**, rules that prohibit sexual intercourse with close blood relatives. But who constitutes a "close blood relative" is a matter of social definition. Consider the case of two young lovers in Seoul, South Korea, whose family names both happen to be Soh. At first the couple gave little thought to the matter, since Koreans have only 249 surnames (for instance, people named Kim account for 20 percent of the 41 million South Koreans). When the Sohs wanted to get married, an inspection of their family registers revealed they had a common ancestor. Both traced their lineage to a

Soh who had lived, 30 generations ago, in the town of Talsong. Under Korean family law, the lovers might as well have been brother and sister. Men and women who share the same name and ancestral village may not marry, since the relationship is considered incestuous. Despite the prohibition, the Sohs married in a civil ceremony. The couple could not legally register their marriage, so the two children born to them were considered illegitimate and ran the risk of being barred from public school. Because of their difficulties, the Sohs recently migrated to the United States (Haberman, 1987).

Incest taboos were once singled out by social scientists as the only universal norm in a world of diverse moral codes. But the sociologist Russell Middleton (1962) found that brother-sister marriage was not only permitted, but frequently practiced, by the ancient Egyptians (Cleopatra was married to two of her younger brothers at different times). He speculates that brother-sister marriages served to maintain the power and property of a family and prevented the splintering of an estate through inheritance. A similar arrangement apparently also occurred among the royal families of Hawaii, the Inca rulers of Peru, and the Dahomey of West Africa. Additionally, the degree of kinship covered by incest varies from society to society. For example, in colonial New England it was incestuous if a man married his deceased wife's sister. But among the ancient Hebrews, the custom of the levirate required that a man marry his brother's widow under some circumstances.

Incestuous relationships are not just prohibited by a society; most people react to them with aversion and disgust. The intensity of such feelings and the worldwide prevalence of incest taboos have led scholars to search for explanations. The psychoanalyst Sigmund Freud (1917) alleged that incest taboos are a psychological reaction against unconscious incestuous desires. The anthropologist Claude Lévi-Strauss (1956) suggested that incest taboos promote alliances between families and reinforce their social interdependence. The anthropologist Bronislaw Malinowski (1927) said that incest taboos prevent destructive sexual jealousies and rivalries within the family. The sociologist Kingsley Davis (1960) contends that incestuous relationships would hopelessly confuse family statuses (for example, the incestuous male offspring of a father-daughter union would be the son of his own sister, a stepson of his own grandmother, and a grandson of his own father). And some anthropologists and sociobiologists, noting that children brought up together avoid sexual relationships and marriage among themselves (such as children raised on Israeli kibbutzim), argue that the behavior is set by genes (Wilson, 1975; Lumsden and Wilson, 1981). These issues remain unresolved, and social scientists continue to find themselves perplexed about the real causes of incest taboos (Dinnage, 1986).

Types of marriage   The relationship between a husband and wife may be structured in one of four ways: **monogamy**, one husband and one wife; **polygyny**, one husband and two or more wives; **polyandry**, two or more husbands and one wife; and **group marriage**, two or more husbands and two or more wives. Monogamy appears in all societies, although other forms may not only be permitted, but preferred. Monogamy was the preferred or ideal type of marriage in less than 20 percent of the 862 societies included in one cross-cultural sample (Murdock, 1967). Not too long ago, members of Western societies believed that monogamy was one of the hallmarks of civilization and that other forms of marriage were signs of barbarism.

Polygyny has enjoyed a wide distribution throughout the world, with 83 percent of the 862 societies permitting husbands to take plural wives. The Old Testament, for example, records polygynous practices among the Hebrews. Gideon's many wives bore him seventy sons; King David had several wives; King Solomon reportedly had seven hundred wives and three hundred concubines; King Solomon's son Rehoboam had eighteen wives and sixty concubines; and Rehoboam's sons also had many wives. As among the ancient Hebrews, it is usually only the economically advantaged males who can afford to have more than one wife. The arrangement is closely tied with economic production and status considerations. Polygyny tends to be favored where large families are advantageous and women make substantial contributions to subsistence (Oliver, 1955; Heath, 1958).

Whereas polygyny has a wide distribution, polyandry is exceedingly rare. Polyandry usually does not represent freedom of sexual choice for women. It often involves the right or the opportunity of younger brothers to have sexual access to the wife of an older brother. Where a family cannot afford wives or marriages for each of its sons, it may find a wife for the eldest son only. The anthropologist W. H. R. Rivers (1906: 515) studied polyandrous practices among the Todas, a non-Hindu people in India, and observed:

> The Todas have a completely organized and definite system of polyandry. When a woman marries a man, it is understood that she becomes the wife of his brothers at the same time. When a boy is married to a girl, not only are his brothers usually regarded as also the husbands of the girl, but any brother born later will similarly be regarded as sharing his older brother's rights. . . . The brothers live together, and my informants seemed to regard it as a ridiculous idea that there should even be disputes or jealousies of the kind that might be expected in such a household. . . . Instead of adultery being regarded as immoral . . . according to the Toda idea, immorality attaches rather to the man who grudges his wife to another.

Social scientists are far from agreement on whether group marriage has ever existed as a cultural norm. There is some evidence that it did occur among the Kaingang of the jungles of Brazil, the Marquesans of the South Pacific, the Chukchee of Siberia, and the Todas of India. At times, as among the Todas, polyandry appears to slip into group marriage when a number of brothers share more than one wife (Stephens, 1963).

Some societies also recognize marriages between individuals of the same sex. The Cheyenne Indians permitted married men to take on *berdaches*, or male transvestites, as second wives (Hoebel, 1960). And the Azande of the African Sudan allowed warriors who could not afford wives to marry "boy-wives" to satisfy their sexual needs. The boy-wives not only had sexual relations with their husbands, but performed many of the chores Azande wives performed for their husbands. Additionally, the husband could sue a lover of his boy-wife in court for adultery (Evans-Pritchard, 1970). Female-female marriages are also found in some African societies, although a sexual relationship is not involved (O'Brien, 1977; Oboler, 1980).

James W. VanderZanden, *The Social Experience: An Introduction to Sociology.* © 1988. Reproduced with permission of The McGraw-Hill Companies.

TASK 3

- GUIDED NOTETAKING
- LISTENING FOR CHRONOLOGY

Listening for Background Information

HISTORY OF THE FAMILY

Listen to the short lecture. It discusses changes in the family at five times in history. As you listen, fill in the table below by writing the major change that occurred at each of the five times. The first one has been done for you.

TIME	MAJOR CHANGE
RURAL, PREINDUSTRIAL	family was self-sufficient; members worked in the home or on the farm to support group
AT THE TIME OF INDUSTRIALIZATION	
DURING THE NINETEENTH CENTURY	
AFTER WORLD WAR II	
TODAY	

Predicting Topics

● PREDICTING AND DISCUSSING
BASED ON TITLES

1. There are three parts to this short magazine article. Look at the titles of the parts. Can you imagine what they are about? Using your own words, write the possible main ideas under each title.

Two Moms and a Baby

Going Home, Again

Blending Two Families

2. Now compare your ideas about the article with those of a partner or two. Have you made the same predictions about the content of each of the parts?

_____

3. In a few words, write your opinion about the ideas you have just discussed concerning the three parts of the article.

Two Moms and a Baby

Going Home, Again

Blending Two Families

TASK 5

- GETTING THE MAIN IDEA
- SUMMARIZING
- EXPRESSING OPINION BASED ON READING

Sharing Information and Opinions About the Topic

A NEW DIVERSITY—THREE SITUATIONS

1. In a group of three, divide the article up. Each person will read only **one** part of it.

   a) In your own words, write important points from your part of the situation in the table below.

TWO MOMS AND A BABY	GOING HOME, AGAIN	BLENDING TWO FAMILIES

   b) Complete the whole table by telling each other the situation you have read. Take notes by listening to each other's points.

2. As a group, discuss your opinions about the situations you have read and discussed. Would these situations occur in your country of origin?

3. What does this information tell you about families in Canada? Write your answer below.

   _____

   _____

   _____

4. Work in a small group. On a separate sheet of paper, list the arguments **in favour of** each of the three situations in the reading. Share your list with the class.

5. Work in the same group. On a separate sheet of paper, list the arguments **against** the situations in the reading. Again, share your list with the class.

Understanding Statistics About the Topic

● REFORMULATING
● DRAWING CONCLUSIONS

Look at the first piece of information in the margin of the article:

52% of respondents agree that they are / were close emotionally to their grandparents; 70 percent say they are close to their pets.

We could rewrite this information in our own words like this:

About half of the people who answered the survey said that they were emotionally close to their grandparents, but 70% said that they were close to their pets.

We could then draw this conclusion:

In general, people feel closer to their pets than to their grandparents.

In a group of three, look at the six other pieces of information in the margin of the article. Working together and using the space below, do the following for each one:

    a) Rewrite it in your own words.

    b) Draw a conclusion from it.

  1. a) Rewrite for the second piece of information:

_____

_____

_____

_____

    b) Conclusion:

_____

_____

_____

  2. a) Rewrite for the third piece of information:

_____

_____

_____

_____

    b) Conclusion:

_____

_____

_____

3. a) Rewrite for the fourth piece of information:

_____

_____

_____

_____

b) Conclusion:

_____

_____

_____

4. a) Rewrite for the fifth piece of information:

_____

_____

_____

_____

b) Conclusion:

_____

_____

_____

5. a) Rewrite for the sixth piece of information:

_____

_____

_____

_____

b) Conclusion:

_____

_____

_____

6. a) Rewrite for the seventh piece of information:

_____

_____

_____

_____

b) Conclusion:

_____

_____

_____

7. Still in your group, take some time to brainstorm the positive and negative implications of each of the seven pieces of information. Write your list on a separate sheet of paper.

8. Separate and form new groups containing one member from each of the original groups. Share your lists of positive and negative implications, and create a master list on a separate sheet of paper.

9. As a class, compare master lists and make sure everyone has the same list.

READING # A New Diversity

Economic and social forces are changing the face of the modern Canadian family

52%

of respondents agree that they are/were close emotionally to their grandparents; 70 percent say they are close to their pets.

61%

of respondents are all-round happy with their family lives. Those who had a happy childhood, hold strong religious beliefs and remain close emotionally to their parents are most likely to fall in the happy category.

26%

of parents disagree with the statement: "It is sometimes acceptable for a parent to spank a child."

TWO MOMS AND A BABY

When it comes to public acceptance of gay rights, the real litmus test is the issue of raising children. Only 37 percent of respondents to the Angus Reid poll disagreed with the statement: "I find nothing wrong with homosexuality." But when asked about same-sex couples raising kids, 67 percent thought it was a bad thing. Those views are familiar to Maureen Mills, 35, and Joanne Beatty, 33, lesbian partners of seven years. They live in South Vancouver with 16-month-old Sydney Beatty Mills, fathered by a male friend and borne by Mills. Some neighbors who accepted the couple's homosexuality, Beatty says, changed when Mills got pregnant: "That really hurt. Some people feel we're not fit to raise a child."

Beatty has no legal rights as a parent, although Mills has specified in her will that, in the event of her death, Sydney should stay with Beatty—a stipulation that could face a legal challenge. And Mills says people tend to question "Joanne's influence. They don't always understand that we have an equal commitment to Sydney's well-being." She calls for legislation that would "legitimize our family status."

For all the negative comments, however, Mills says that they have heard even more positive ones. And although they worry about the social stigma Sydney might face, they have no second thoughts. "I think it's important to be visible," says Mills. "That way, people may learn that we have more commonality than differences with other parents."

—ADRIENNE WEBB *IN VANCOUVER*

GOING HOME, AGAIN

Dave Walsh never expected to be living with his parents, never mind his in-laws, at the age of 25. But after graduating from the University of Alberta in Edmonton with a civil engineering degree last year, he faced the bleakest job market since the 1930s. Unemployed and burdened with hefty student loans, Walsh and his new wife, Carolin Henry—who earns only a modest income as a social worker—moved in with her parents in Hamilton after their marriage last July. "I was brought up to believe that when you get married, you have your own place," says Walsh. But it was simply not possible. "We asked them to stay here because we knew that they couldn't manage on their own," says Carolin's mother, Aldith Henry. She and her husband, Joel, had already helped support

71%

of respondents say that the use of reproductive technology to allow people to give birth will have a positive impact on families and society.

53%

of those married or common-law couples who reported being dissatisfied with their relationships said they would like to improve "communication." Only eight percent of the dissatisfied couples said that they wanted to improve their sex lives. Parents of young children were an exception—15 percent of them wanted improved sexual relations with their spouses.

10%

of never-married respondents have given birth to, or fathered, at least one child; so have half the people now living common law.

82%

of respondents who are living with a common-law partner consider their living arrangement to be a "family."

another adult son, Jimmy, who moved back into his old room for two years when he could not find a job after graduating from college in 1990. And the family's experience is not unique. According to the Angus Reid poll, about one in five adults over the age of 24 live with their parents. "It's tough for young people today," says Aldith Henry. "We don't like them to struggle."

Hard times are bringing families like the Henrys together—for better or for worse. Walsh is grateful for his in-laws' help and they, in turn, praise him and Carolin for pitching in. At the same time, the parents, who want to see their adult children become established, are increasingly concerned. "We did it with a good heart," adds Aldith Henry. "But it isn't always easy." Joel Henry, 47, works long hours at his motor mechanics shop and his wife, 56, works full time as a nurse to help pay off the mortgage and put their younger son, Paul, through university.

And most twentysomethings yearn for independence. Space was not a problem in the Henry's five-bedroom house, but Walsh sometimes felt that inviting friends over "would impose on the rest of the family." Walsh recently found part-time work as a laborer while he continues his search for an engineering job. Two weeks ago, he and his wife moved to a nearby townhouse. "It's going to be a financial strain," says Walsh. "But we can't grow as close as we want to if we don't have privacy."

—SHARON DOYLE DREIDGER

BLENDING TWO FAMILIES

Only a few weeks before François Cantin married Louise Thériault last August, Cantin reached an agreement with his first wife that gave him custody of their two young children. Louis-Philippe, 8, and Maude, 6, moved from their mother's place in the country to the Cantin-Thériault household in Quebec City. "It's been quite an eye-opener," says Thériault, a 30-year-old graphic designer with no children of her own. "François has to work a lot of overtime and I work at home, so I find myself almost like a single mother sometimes." Thériault took on much of the responsibility for the children. And it has not all gone smoothly. "I had a very frank discussion with the boy recently because his attitude was really bad," she says. "I told him I took care of him and his sister only because I wanted to, not because I had to." She also told Louis-Philippe that she loved him—and that it was OK for him to love her, as well as his mother, a concept he had struggled with. But while that discussion helped, the transition into a blended family, combined with Louis-Philippe's difficulty in adapting to life in the city, was just too much for the boy. This month, he is moving back to his mother's home in the country.

In an age of rising divorce rates, blended families are increasingly common. About 343,400—or seven percent of all Canadian families raising children—include at least one stepchild, according to the Vanier Institute of the Family in Ottawa. And such families—afflicted, sometimes, by the acrimony of divorce as well as by centuries-old stereotypes about wicked stepmothers—face particular challenges. "People must remember that love and respect in blended families is not instantaneous," says Montreal psychologist Liliane Spector. "Sometimes it can take years, and sometimes the best you can hope for is a civil relationship." Blended families, adds Spector, are not like traditional ones, and must define completely new roles; which parent has responsibility for discipline, who does the chores, who pays for what.

Often, they must also struggle to forge bonds between new siblings. "That was the big problem in our case," says Michel Vermette, a 35-year-old Canada Post employee in Quebec City. Two years ago, his girlfriend, Sonya St-Gelais, 35, and her now-14-year-old son moved in with Vermette and his two children, a boy aged 16 and a girl of 12. The children did not get along. "Michel and I," says St-Gelais, "found ourselves playing the police all the time while the kids screamed injustice." Within six months, St-Gelais and her son moved out, although she and Vermette are still dating. "We plan to try living together again," says Vermette—"after the kids turn 18."

—MARK CARDWELL IN QUEBEC CITY

Getting Specific Information About the Topic

- PREDICTING THROUGH DISCUSSION
- SKIMMING FOR THE MAIN IDEA
- SUMMARIZING
- EXPRESSING OPINION BASED ON READING

CHILDFREE MARRIAGES

The next reading is taken from a sociology textbook on marriage and the family in Canada.

1. With a partner, discuss whether or not you feel that child-free marriages are popular in Canada. Estimate what percentage of marriages are childless in Canada.

2. Divide the two questions (a) and (b) below between you. Separate to join a new partner who has chosen the same question.

   a) What types of couples are likely to be childless by choice? Reach an agreement and fill in the table below with your responses to create a profile of a typical childless couple.

URBAN/RURAL	EDUCATION LEVEL	INCOME LEVEL

   b) Discuss the effect of childlessness on married couples. Are they happy? Are they active? Are they satisfied with their marriage? Write the main points of your discussion here:

3. With your original partner, share the results of your discussions.

4. Take ten minutes to skim the reading. Compare the information in the reading to your discussion results. Briefly list the information from discussion and reading in the table below.

DISCUSSION	READING

5. Write a few sentences to compare the information from the reading and the discussion. What is similar? What is different?

_____

_____

_____

_____

6. Make a brief list below of the **positive** and **negative** aspects of childfree marriage.

The traditional assumption that family formation follows marriage is no longer universally held in most Western societies including Canada. In her pioneering study of voluntarily childless couples, Veevers (1980) estimated that about five to seven percent of married couples opt for childlessness. However, her estimate seems to be rather conservative given the recent data which suggest that about 20 percent of married or cohabiting couples in Canada may never have children. Veevers tended to characterize voluntary childlessness as a *deviant* phenomenon but given its widespread occurrence, it has clearly become a *variant* marital pattern in Canada.

Who are these Canadians who negate the dominant pronatalist approach to life? Based on Veevers' (1980) and other studies (e.g., Ramu, 1984; Ramu and Tavuchis, 1986), the following profile is constructed. The vast majority of childless couples live in urban areas. They tend to be better educated than average, and to earn higher incomes than is average for the population and this is mainly because both spouses tend to be employed. They marry late and may postpone several times the birth of their first child until they finally decide not to have any children. Childfree wives tend to be first born or born into a large family.

They generally do not subscribe to religion and seldom attend church or church-related activities.

The childfree wives tend to believe in self-actualization and this prompts them to trade maternity for occupational success. Because of their commitment to professional advancement, childfree wives feel that they neither have the time nor the necessary resources to raise children successfully. The choice to be childless is not perceived by such couples as an act against parenthood—it is just that parenthood is not for them. Furthermore, childless spouses favour an intense couple-centred relationship rather than diffused family solidarity.

Opting for childlessness has some tangible consequences for couples as studies have shown (e.g., Veevers, 1980). For example, those couples with few domestic encumbrances enjoy greater freedom than do those who opt for parenthood. Such freedom may be used to participate in recreational activities, or to upgrade their educational skills which, in turn, facilitates occupational success, especially for wives. Finally, virtually all studies have noted that childless couples enjoy a significantly higher level of marital satisfaction than do those who have embraced parenthood (Veevers, 1980; Lupri and Frideres, 1981; Ramu, 1984).

"Marital Patterns in Canada," George Kurian. In *Marriage and the Family in Canada Today*, Second Edition, Ed. G.N. Ramu, © 1993. Used by permission of Prentice Hall Canada Inc.

TASK 8

More Specific Information About the Topic

- PREDICTING
- GETTING THE MAIN IDEA
- SUMMARIZING

SINGLE-PARENT FAMILIES

1. In a group of four, divide the four numbered paragraphs of this reading, taken from a sociology textbook, among you.

2. Predict the type of information you expect from a textbook reading on single-parent families in Canada. What types of statistics and descriptive information do you expect to find here? Make a few notes in the space below.

3. Read the paragraph assigned to you. Give it a title and make a few short notes below on the most important facts discussed.

4. Without referring back to the text, take turns to present your paragraph to the group. On a separate sheet of paper, make notes on the titles and information you hear.

5. Read the entire text in five minutes. Clear up any missing or inaccurate information from your notes or from the discussion.

6. On a separate sheet of paper, write a one-paragraph summary describing the typical single-parent family.

7. Share your summary with the members of your group. Do you all agree on the typical family? Clear up any differences in your summaries.

Just as marriages can take a number of alternative forms, so too can families. The largest increases in the 1980s have in fact involved nontraditional family forms, including common-law unions and single-parent families. Together, these two forms made up 22.8 percent of families in the 1991 census.

1. Families with only one parent made up 13 percent of all families in 1991 but they vary considerably according to the age, marital status, and sex of the parent. In 1971 most one-parent families were led by a widowed parent. In contrast, in 1986 those with a separated or divorced parent made up 59.5 percent of the total, while another 13.4 percent had a never-married parent (Ram, 1990: 87). Only 17.8 percent of the one-parent families were led by a male parent, while the rest—the vast majority—were headed by women.

2. Over the course of their life, in fact, the experience of single parenthood is quite common for women. In 1984, among women between 18 and 64 who ever had children, 26 percent had experienced lone parenthood. For about two-thirds of these, parenting alone had ended either through a new union (the great majority) or when the children left home (16 percent). The average duration of the lone-parenting episodes was 5.5 years, with 10 percent lasting less than 6 months and 17 percent lasting more than 10 years. Among those who experienced one episode, 12 percent experienced at least one subsequent episode (Moore, 1989a).

3. An increasingly common route into single parenthood involves births to single women. Such births have increased over the period 1975–1986. The largest increases have occurred not among teenagers, whose birth and abortion rates have actually declined since the 1970s (Grindstaff, 1990), but among women over the age of 30, again evidence of the separation between sexual activity and marriage. On the other hand, many of these women may in fact be living in common-law unions and thus may not really be single parents (Ram, 1990: 32).

4. Moore (1987) has analyzed female lone parenting with the help of the 1984 *Family History Survey*. Compared with currently married women of the same age, female lone parents are more likely to have lived in common-law relationships, to have had their children earlier, and to have less education. In effect, they must raise children while facing a double disadvantage of lack of support from a spouse and fewer job skills. McQuillan (1992) found that between 1971 and 1986, as participation of married women in the labor force increased, the income gap between single-parent and two-parent families grew. Thus, along with the greater incidence of elderly females living alone cited earlier, the growth in the number of young, female-led, single-parent families has contributed considerably to the feminization of poverty in Canada.

Basic Sociology: A Canadian Introduction, Fifth Edition, Eds. James J. Teevan and W.E. Hewitt, © 1995. Used by permission of Prentice Hall Canada Inc.

Debate

1. As a class, discuss the structure and aims of a debate.

2. Discuss and select **one** aspect of family life that you have dealt with in this unit.

3. In small groups, write a single-sentence **motion** for debate. A motion is the point that is to be argued. As a class, choose the best motion statement for the debate.

4. As a class, select a maximum of six members for each debating team and four judges.

5. The debating teams should meet to decide the following:
   a) main arguments for their side, as well as support for each main argument
   b) key arguments the other side will likely make
   c) order of speakers on the team
   d) contents of the team's opening statement

6. The judges should meet to decide the following:
   a) criteria for deciding the winning side
   b) key arguments to expect from each side

If possible, the judges should take some time to listen in on the teams discussing their strategy.

7. When the debating teams and the judges are ready, the debate may begin. Follow these procedures:
   a) Time the speakers carefully. The first speaker on each side making the team's opening statement is allowed three minutes. Other speakers are allowed two minutes each.
   b) Flip a coin to decide which team goes first. The speakers will then alternate between teams.
   c) Take a minute between speakers to discuss strategy.

8. At the end, the judges will first present a summary of the debate to the class. They will then deliver their judgement and their reasons for it.

USE THE NEXT PAGE TO HELP PLAN THE DEBATE.

MOTION:

_____

_____

_____

_____

ARGUMENT 1

Support

ARGUMENT 2

Support

ARGUMENT 3

Support

ARGUMENT 4

Support

NOTES DURING DEBATE

6 Sleep: Are We Getting Enough?

This unit focuses on sleep and sleep deprivation—whether or not people get enough sleep and what happens if they don't. It involves reading about how sleep works, and the personal and social consequences of a lack of sleep. It also gives scientific information about how sleep is linked with some very important aspects of health. The unit leads to a lot of discussion as you share information from the reading.

The final project in this unit is to conduct a survey about the consequences of sleep deprivation and to write a short report about the topic. To prepare, you will try to organize the information from the unit to create a framework for the survey and report.

You should turn to the project description at the end of the unit regularly to see how much information and how many skills you need to help you complete it.

READING *You will read for complete information, skim and scan academic text, and analyse information paragraph by paragraph to get the most important information for your purposes.*

LISTENING *You will take notes on a lecture by following an outline.*

WRITING *You will write short answers to tasks presented in the unit. You will write a brief report in a step-by-step way, collaborating with classmates.*

SPEAKING *You will discuss your opinions and information presented in the unit. You will talk and work together to conduct the survey and write the final report.*

TO BEGIN, TURN THE PAGE AND START THINKING ABOUT AND DISCUSSING THE TOPIC IN GENERAL.

Introduction to the Topic

● SHARING PERSONAL AND
BACKGROUND INFORMATION

Answer the following questions. Discuss your answers in a group of three.

1. How many hours of sleep did you get on an average night in your country or when you were living with your family?

   _____ 7

2. How many hours of sleep have you been getting on an average night lately?

   _____ 6.30
   9/30

3. Do you feel that you get enough sleep? How many hours of sleep does a person normally need?

   _____

   _____

   _____

4. Do you ever sleep during the day?

   _____

   _____

5. Is sleeping during the day common in your country or family?

   _____

   _____

6. Have you seen people sleeping during the day here in Canada?

   _____

   _____

7. Do you feel that napping is a good thing or not? Explain.

   _____

   _____

   _____

8. What are the consequences of sleep deprivation or insufficient hours of sleep?

   _____

   _____

   _____

Getting Specific Information About the Topic

● PREDICTING
● SCANNING FOR SPECIFICS

1. Before reading the following excerpt from a psychology textbook, take a few minutes as a class to brainstorm a list of mental and physical consequences of lack of sleep.

2. Scan the reading and write a list of the consequences of sleep deprivation. Compare it to your brainstorming list.

3. Why is REM sleep important?

_____

_____

_____

_____

_____

_____

4. What are the consequences of lack of REM sleep?

_____

_____

_____

_____

_____

_____

Sleep is an element in our lives whose importance should not be underestimated. On one occasion or another, you have probably had to try to function on an inadequate amount of sleep. If at such times you suffered from fatigue, headaches, and poor concentration, you know from personal experience just how damaging a lack of sleep can be to you.

The scientific evidence on sleep deprivation confirms that adequate sleep is necessary for most of us to function effectively. Research has shown that total or even partial sleep deprivation may produce difficulty in concentration, childish behavior, poor reality contact, aggressiveness, reduced interpersonal effectiveness, poor performance on various kinds of laboratory tasks, reduced motivation, hallucinations, and severe psychological disturbance (Webb, 1973). However, the impact of sleep deprivation is highly variable. Some people can handle lengthy periods without sleep and show relatively few ill effects (Ross, 1965). Furthermore, there is evidence that too *much* sleep may lead to fatigue and inept performance on tasks requiring alertness (Taub & Burger, 1969). The link between lack of sleep and physical health is only modestly problematic because sleep deprivation has a self-limiting quality. Generally, people can go only so long without sleep, so that massive sleep deprivation is relatively unusual. Nonetheless, there is evidence (Palmblad, 1981) to support the notion that sleep deprivation reduces the effectiveness of our immune response, making us more vulnerable to infectious agents.

REM sleep. The sheer amount of sleep that you get is not the only important consideration. It appears that the *kind* of sleep that you get may also be relevant. Scientists have discovered that after we fall asleep, we go through a series of stages, during which the quality of our sleep changes. Typically, sleep is divided into five stages, which most of us revolve through in a cyclical fashion about four times each night. A rather special, deep stage of sleep (that is, a stage from which it is difficult to awaken you) is commonly called **REM sleep**. REM is an abbreviation for "rapid eye movements." One of the more noticeable signs of this stage of sleep is rapid, lateral eye movements that take place beneath the closed eyelids. This stage of sleep is also accompanied by relatively little muscular activity and large fluctuations in autonomic functions. Interestingly, it appears that *most* dreaming occurs during this stage, and your brain activity, as measured by an **electroencephalograph**, is surprisingly similar to that displayed while awake (Webb, 1973).

REM deprivation. Of interest to us is the evidence that a lack of REM sleep may have detrimental effects similar to those of *total* sleep deprivation. Dement (1960) monitored sleep activity and prevented subjects from getting any REM sleep by awakening them just as they went into the REM stage. These subjects were able to get a reasonable amount of sleep (in other stages) but were deprived of REM sleep. Surprisingly, the REM deprivation led to negative effects such as heightened irritability, anxiety, and fatigue. This evidence suggests that not only do we need sleep, we also need "good quality" sleep, including a certain amount of REM sleep. Most adults spend about 20% of their total sleep time in the REM stage (Webb & Agnew, 1968). Although this exact proportion is not essential for everyone, it is clear that the task of getting proper sleep is more complex than most people realize.

REM SLEEP. A deep stage of sleep, during which there are rapid lateral eye movements beneath the closed eyelids; the stage of sleep during which most dreaming occurs.

ELECTROENCEPHALOGRAPH (EEG). An elaborate electronic device used to record the electrical activity of the brain. Electrodes are attached to the scalp, and the recorded electrical activity is translated into line tracings, which are commonly called brain waves.

TASK 3

More Specific Information

● READING FOR COMPLETE INFORMATION
● SUMMARIZING

1. The next text is part of a book about sleep, excerpted in a magazine. Follow the first part of this reading paragraph by paragraph, answering the questions below.

a) What do the title and subtitle of the article suggest?

_____

_____

_____

_____

b) What is the purpose of the story told in the first paragraph?

_____

_____

_____

_____

c) What question is being answered in paragraph 3?

_____

_____

_____

d) According to paragraph 4, what do we discover when comparing ape and human sleep? What does this comparison imply?

_____

_____

_____

_____

_____

e) What can we conclude from the studies discussed in paragraph 5?

_____

_____

_____

_____

_____

f) Paragraph 6 describes a research study. What did the study conclude?

_____

_____

_____

_____

2. Now read the rest of the text to answer the questions below.

a) What is **daylight-saving time**?

_____

_____

_____

_____

b) What does the traffic accident data from daylight-saving time tell us?

_____

_____

_____

_____

c) How much did the United States pay as a society in 1988 for lack of sleep?

_____

_____

d) How many days of productive work in the United States were lost in 1988 due to lack of sleep?

_____

e) What was different about the sleep patterns of Abraham de Moivre and Thomas Edison?

_____

_____

_____

3. With a partner, compare your answers. Together, on a separate sheet of paper, prepare a written summary of the negative effects of sleep deprivation on individuals and society. Share your summary with another pair and clear up any differences with reference to the text.

Sleep Sliding Away

BY STANLEY COREN

We're a sleep-deprived society, and the carnage after daylight-saving time proves it

1. It is now 8:30 p.m. and I am sitting in the Orpheum Theatre in Vancouver. It is filled with many of the hard-driving, ambitious people who occupy the upper economic strata of the city. The man to my left is talking about a court case he is working on, and two men behind me are discussing a stock issue. Obviously, business has not been left behind this night. The formally dressed ushers have closed the heavy doors, and the lights are dimmed. The Vancouver Symphony Orchestra has just started a typical weeknight concert. The melodic sounds of a piece by Debussy fill the hall, and the audience grows quiet and seems to relax noticeably. By the third movement it seems that every fourth person is asleep, despite the hefty thirty-dollar cost of a ticket for the orchestra seat they are occupying.

2. The scene at the symphony is typical. As Dr. David F. Dinges, a biological psychologist at the Institute for Experimental Psychiatry in Philadelphia, has said, "I can't think of a single study that hasn't found people getting less sleep than they ought to." When I looked at seven of the larger and more recent surveys that measured sleep length in North American and European adults, the average was around seven hours and twenty minutes. If this is too little, how much sleep should we be getting?

3. There are a number of ways that we might look for this answer. One of the ways is to consider the sleep patterns of animals that are closely related to human beings. When we do this we find that most of the apes and monkeys have a circadian rhythm that is similar to that of humans, and a sleep-wake cycle that is similar to that of people who live in cultures where the siesta is still practised. Specifically, these animals have a long sleep at night and a shorter sleep in midafternoon. Let's define total sleep time per day as any night-time sleep plus any day naps or siestas, rounded off to the nearest hour. For monkeys (specifically, the baboon, rhesus monkey, and squirrel monkey), total sleep time is ten hours. Of the great apes, our closest evolutionary cousins, the chimpanzee sleeps the same ten hours as the monkeys, and the gorilla's total rounds off to twelve hours of sleep.

4. Does monkey or ape sleep predict anything about human sleep? Man and the apes have many more similarities than differences. Apes have the same internal organs and similar nervous systems and brains, can eat similar foods, are susceptible to the same diseases, and even suffer from many of the same physiological difficulties. Recent molecular genetic analyses have shown that the degree of similarity between man and chimpanzee is ninety-eight per cent. Electrically, the sleep stages in man and the other primates are virtually identical. With that in mind we can sensibly speculate that there should also be some similarity between humans and apes in terms of their sleep needs. Given the fact that, without exception, all the apes and monkeys studied to date sleep ten hours or more each day, we might conclude that human beings are sleeping around two and a half hours less than they should.

5. Several studies conducted by Wilse Webb and H.W. Agnew have confirmed our need to sleep longer under very controlled conditions. These researchers tested people who were sleeping in experimental chambers designed to eliminate any hints as to the time of day. Volunteers were placed on a rigidly controlled sleep schedule that allowed them eight hours in bed each night for ten nights, followed by ten nights when they could sleep as long as they liked. This group ended up sleeping approximately nine hours each for the entire second ten-day period, clearly confirming that eight hours of sleep is not enough as a regular sleep diet.

6. If we need more than seven and a half hours of sleep, then increasing normal sleep length for people who have no complaints about daytime sleepiness ought to show some daytime benefits. This was demonstrated by Timothy Roehrs and Thomas Roth and their associates at the Sleep Disorders Research Center of the Henry Ford Hospital in Detroit. In one of their experiments, for example, they extended the time in bed for their volunteers to ten hours a night, which was two hours longer than their previous sleep time. This extended sleep length was continued for six days. The daytime alertness of the participants in this test was measured using the Multiple Sleep Latency Test, which is a measure of how long it takes a person to fall asleep under quiet conditions at various times during the day. Increasing the sleep length immediately increased the daytime alertness of these male volunteers, with the greatest improvement coming for those individuals who initially showed the greatest amount of sleepiness.

Is there any way to demonstrate that sleep loss is a major culprit that has a negative effect on our everyday lives?

The answer came one April evening. I was getting ready to go to bed when my wife asked me, "Did you remember to reset the clocks?"

"Why?" I asked.

"We're shifting to daylight-saving time," she said.

"Sometimes God smiles on researchers," I thought to myself.

Daylight-saving time, which is also called "summer time" in some countries, is a system in use by around thirty nations in the world today. It involves advancing clocks in the spring or summer to extend the hours of natural daylight obtainable during our usual waking hours, and then returning to standard time in the fall.

Daylight-saving time was exactly what I needed. It was a situation where the entire population of North America would all lose one hour of sleep on the same night in April and would all have the opportunity to sleep one hour extra in the fall. If an hour's worth of sleep loss caused noticeable negative effects in the population, we would know that our sleep debt as a population is large enough to mean that we are potentially teetering on the edge of major problems.

But I needed some measure of inefficiency or error or lack of judgment. What I really needed was day-by-day data on accidents. My university's data librarian, after a long and tedious search, somehow found the one person at Transport Canada who could provide appropriate data on traffic accidents.

Eight weeks later I had data representing every reported vehicle accident in Canada in 1991 and 1992, with information as to the province and the specific date that the accident occurred. We had a total of better than a million and a half accidents from all over Canada. There was one minor quirk, however. We had to leave out data from the province of Saskatchewan, which never accepted the concept of daylight-saving time. I looked at the number of traffic accidents on the Monday immediately following the shift to daylight-saving time and compared this to the Monday before and the Monday after.

I was ecstatic. I don't believe the results could be clearer. Immediately following the spring daylight-saving-time shift, when we lose an hour of sleep, there is approximately a seven percent increase in traffic accidents, and this increase is gone a week later. Presumably, the increase comes about simply because the additional hour of sleep debt makes us that much more inattentive and clouds our judgment a bit more. In the fall, when we gain an additional hour of sleep, the pattern is reversed. Immediately after the daylight-saving-time shift there is a decrease in the number of traffic accidents of approximately seven percent, but a week later things are back to "normal." Presumably, the decrease is because that extra hour of sleep nibbles away at our existing sleep debt and makes our attention a bit better and our judgment a bit more accurate.

These data tell us a lot about our current sleep-debt status. As a society, we must be running a fairly heavy sleep debt if the loss of one hour more of sleep can make it seven percent more likely that we will have a mishap on the road. Remember, these are only the events we can count and tabulate. How many minor accidents happened at home or on the job because of a microsleep or lapse in attention? How many design errors were missed, computer-program steps miscoded, and prescriptions improperly filled?

The direct monetary cost of sleep deprivation and the accidents it produces is much greater than most people can possibly imagine. For example, Dr. Damien Leger prepared a report on the cost of sleep-related accidents in the U.S. National Commission on Sleep Disorders. The results of his calculations are sobering and astounding. Leger reports that in 1988 the cost of motor-vehicle accidents caused by sleepiness was $37.9-billion; to this we must add the costs of sleep-induced accidents in public transportation, which is another $720-million. The cost of work-related accidents caused by sleepiness was $133.34-billion. Accidents in public places, including falls, that were directly due to sleepiness came to $1.34-billion, while accidents around the home due to sleep deficits resulted in a cost of $2.72-billion. The total cost of sleep-related accidents in 1988 was $56.02-billion.

Although the dollar cost is appalling, the human cost is even more significant. In 1988, in the U.S., a total of 24,318 deaths resulted from accidents related to sleepiness. In addition, there were 2,474,430 disabling injuries resulting from accidents in which the decreased mental efficiency and attentiveness due to sleep loss were the major underlying factors. Sleepiness-related on-the-job injuries resulted in 29,250,000 workdays lost in 1988 (with 13,650,000 days lost owing to the accident itself and 15,600,000 days lost owing to complications and long-term effects of the accident within the first year). Off-the-job accidents took a toll of 23,400,000 workdays lost, giving a total of work- plus non-work-related accidents of 52,650,000. All this was the time lost in 1988, the year the sleep-related accidents occurred; of course, when accidents are severe and disabling, they often continue to have an impact on the person's life for years to come. Pain, complications, resultant diseases, and late-occurring effects may cause work loss for years after an accident. Using Leger's figures we can estimate that the accidents that occurred in 1988 will have later time lost on the job amounting to 152,000,000 workdays. If we total the time lost in 1988 due to sleep-related accidents, we end up with the astonishing figure of 204,650,000 days of productive work lost to the United States economy because of only one year's worth of sleep-related accidents.

Given the data showing that inadequate sleep is probably at the source of many errors, misjudgments, accidents, and deaths, it is a truly odd feature of our society that short sleepers are idolized. We are continually reminded of the great figures who slept very little, including Napoleon, Winston Churchill, John F. Kennedy, Salvador Dali, and Leonardo da Vinci.

Whenever a longer than usual pattern is found in a respected person, it is almost always apologized for, as if the biographer were ashamed of its existence. The British mathematician Abraham de Moivre was one of the groundbreaking workers in the fields of probability theory and trigonometry. He was said to have always been a long sleeper, and the length of his sleep seems to have increased in his old age. De Moivre's biographers are always quick to point out that he was a genius who made many mathematical discoveries despite his long sleeping habits. Thomas Edison—who held that sleep was a waste of time and that too much sleep was harmful to a person's health—even used de Moivre as an object lesson: "One day he slept right up to the limit of 24 hours, and that finished him. He died in his sleep. Too much sleep is unhealthy, and Moivre proves that it can kill you."

Of course, Edison and his biographers always pointed out that Edison, himself, was a very short sleeper. The truth of the matter is that Edison, like most of the short sleepers in history, probably had such a strong work ethic that he simply repressed or underestimated the length of time he spent napping to make up for his shortened night-time hours of sleep. The auto maker Henry Ford once made an unexpected visit to Edison's lab. One of the technicians stopped him from entering Edison's private office, noting that "Mr. Edison is taking a nap."

Ford thought this was amusing and said, "I understood that Mr. Edison didn't sleep very much."

"Oh, that's true," said the technician. "He doesn't sleep very much at all, he just naps a lot."

Sleep is simply not <u>dispensable</u>, regardless of the attempts in today's society to treat it as if it were merely unproductive "down time." The desire to get more sleep is not a sign of laziness, nor does it represent a lack of ambition. The need for sleep is real, and the idea that one can go without sleep is wrong. Perhaps it is time for policy makers, health workers, and all the rest of us to wake up.

Reprinted with the permission of The Free Press, a division of Simon & Schuster, from *Sleep Thieves: An Eye-Opening Exploration into the Science and Mysteries of Sleep* by Stanley Coren. Copyright © 1996 by Stanley Coren.

TASK 4

Deepening Understanding

● GUIDED NOTETAKING

THE INTERNAL CLOCK

Listen to the lecture carefully, filling in the outline below with point-form notes.

1. Clock day

2. Internal clock

   a) Research from 1960s

     • What happened

     • What it proves

   b) Later laboratory research

3. Shift work

   a) Traditional shift change system

   b) System following the internal clock

4. A way to help people adjust to changes in time rhythms

5. Benefit of sleep research

TASK 5
Testing Ability to Get Specific Information

● READING FOR COMPLETE
  UNDERSTANDING

THE HEALING POWER OF SLEEP

Read the following newspaper article and answer the questions below. You have 30 minutes to finish. Check your score out of 28 points after discussing the answers as a class.

1. What is the main idea of the reading? (1 point)

   _____

   _____

   _____

2. What is the purpose of the situations presented in the first paragraph? (1 point)

   _____

   _____

   _____

   _____

3. Complete the table below with information about REM and non-REM sleep. (3 points)

	REM SLEEP	NON-REM SLEEP
CHARACTERISTICS		
PURPOSE		not fully understood

4. What is the cause of death of the rats in total sleep deprivation studies? (2 points)

_____

_____

_____

5. What happened to the immune systems of human subjects in sleep deprivation studies? (1 point)

_____

_____

_____

6. How do researchers think that daytime fatigue in AIDS patients may be explained? (2 points)

_____

_____

_____

7. a) What organ of the body may be responsible for promoting or controlling sleep? (1 point)

_____

b) How does it do so? (1 point)

_____

_____

_____

_____

8. Name three possible purposes of sleep. (3 points)

a) _____

b) _____

c) _____

9. Fill in the missing statements to document Dr. Allan Rechtschaffen's and Dr. Carol Everson's research. (4 points)

a) Two rats were put into the same environment.

b) _____

_____

_____

c) The rat deprived of sleep began to lose weight after two weeks, in spite of eating heavily.

d) _____

_____

_____

e) Sleep-deprived rats resembled cancer patients: weakened and wasted, but with normal blood, urine, and organs.

f) _____

_____

_____

g) These infections did not damage tissue.

h) _____

_____

_____

i) Further tests are underway to measure immune-response in these situations.

10. What possible conclusion could be drawn from the discovery that medical students, caretakers of Alzheimer's patients, and bereaved people have reduced T cell and B cell counts? (2 points)

_____

_____

_____

_____

_____

11. Complete the table below to show what Dr. David Dinges discovered in his research into healthy people who suffered sleep loss. (3 points)

TYPE OF CELL	PURPOSE	REACTION
T cells and B cells		no change
	act when body has an unknown invader	

12. a) According to Dr. James Krueger's theory of sleep, what chemicals are released during sleep? (1 point)

_____

_____

b) What purpose do these chemicals serve? (1 point)

_____

_____

13. What are two possible implications of this sleep research for the treatment of human disease? (2 points)

a) _____

b) _____

THE HEALING POWER OF SLEEP

New findings suggest the immune system is recharged during sleep

BY SANDRA BLAKESLEE
Citizen news services

A college student goes two nights without sleep to cram for exams and on the third day comes down with a cold. A night-shift employee begins working days and gets the flu. A surgery patient who is awakened four times a night in the hospital begins to recover only after going home and getting a good night's sleep.

Are these situations coincidental? Or do they show that sleep loss promotes illness? Despite intense interest in the question, sleep researchers have been hard pressed to show exactly how sleep influences human health and disease.

But now a burst of findings is beginning to shed light on the ultimate purpose of sleep, and in particular on the convoluted interplay between sleep and the immune system.

Experiments suggest that the immune system is somehow repaired or bolstered during sleep and that it, in turn, has a role in regulating sleep.

Sleep is divided into periods of so-called REM sleep, characterized by rapid eyeball movements and dreaming, and longer periods of non-REM sleep. Neither kind of sleep is at all well understood, but REM sleep is assumed to serve some restorative function of the brain. The purpose of non-REM sleep is even more mysterious. The new experiments, such as those described for the first time at a recent meeting of the Society for Sleep Research in Minneapolis, suggest intriguing explanations for the purpose of non-REM sleep.

For example, it has long been known that total sleep deprivation is 100-percent lethal to rats, yet, upon autopsy, the animals look completely normal. A researcher has now solved the mystery of why the animals die. The rats develop bacterial infections of the blood, as if their immune systems had crashed.

In another study, healthy men and women were deprived of sleep for three days while their blood was monitored for immune system factors. Researchers expected to see a decline in immune function, yet the opposite happened. The subjects' immune system went into overdrive, seeming to respond to sleep deprivation as if it were an invading organism like a bacterium or virus.

In a study of AIDS patients, researchers found abnormal fluctuations of an immune system chemical that in healthy people is released rhythmically during sleep. The abnormality may help explain debilitating daytime fatigue in AIDS.

This immune factor may also be related to a nightly rhythmic contraction of the small intestine, researchers said, raising the distinct possibility that the intestine sends a sleep-promoting signal to the brain via the immune system. In this view, the bowel may be telling the brain to go to sleep so that it and other organs can carry out housekeeping functions.

Sleep serves many purposes, said Dr. Harvey Moldofsky, director of the University of Toronto Centre for Sleep and Chronobiology. Apparently, animals sleep to regulate body temperature, organize memories and replenish the immune system, he said. But most research has focussed on sleep as a brain phenomenon, ignoring the rest of the body. The cells, organs, hormones and immune factors in the periphery may, like the brain, contain molecular clocks that help drive daily sleep and wake cycles, he said.

Some of the new research began with a mystery that presented itself 10 years ago. Dr. Allan Rechtschaffen at the University of Chicago Sleep Research Laboratory put two rats into the same environment, but permitted only one to sleep. No striking differences emerged until the end of the second week, when the sleep-deprived rat began to gorge itself on food yet grew skinnier and skinnier without exercising more. After one more week, the sleep-deprived rat lost the ability to regulate its body temperature and died.

Later, in looking for the cause of death of sleep-deprived rats in many such experiments, researchers could find nothing wrong with them. Their organs, blood and urine all seemed normal. The animals resembled cancer patients whose bodies are either weakened by chemotherapy or wasting away from their disease, said Dr. Carol Everson, a senior staff fellow at the National Institute of Mental Health in Bethesda, Md., and a former student of Rechtschaffen's.

"I began thinking, what could be toxic? Maybe the rats were infected," she said. After culturing their blood, Everson found that the rats had died from bacterial infections of the blood. The bacteria were strains that the animals were in contact with every day, she said, and do not normally cause disease.

Oddly, these infections did not damage tissue, Everson said, suggesting that the rats' immune systems did not mount an aggressive attack on the bacteria. Further tests are under way to measure the immune response during the sleep-deprivation experiments, she said.

Meanwhile, Dr. David Dinges, a psychiatrist at the University of Pennsylvania, is testing the effects of sleep deprivation on healthy men and women. There is a long-held belief, based on very little evidence, that going without sleep will make you sick, Dinges said. Some studies have shown that medical students taking exams, caretakers of patients with Alzheimer's disease and people in bereavement have reduced lymphocyte counts—the T cells and B cells that combat infection—and decreases in other immune system cells, he said. The idea is that people in crisis who may not be sleeping well have depressed immune systems.

But few studies have looked at how healthy people respond to sleep loss, Dinges said. In an ambitious experiment that is now being analysed, Dinges and his colleagues recruited 24 healthy volunteers who agreed to live in a sleep lab for one week. Dinges said that he and others expected to find a decline in immune function after sleep loss. "But from the start," he said, "we realized we were on to something different."

The T cells and B cells that are called upon to attack specific pathogens showed no change, he said. But monocytes, granulocytes and natural killer cells—immune cells that are called into play when the body responds to an unknown invader—went sky-high.

The sleep-deprived subjects seem to be mounting what immunologists call a non-specific host response, Dinges said. It is a first line of defence against disease-causing agents and means that these people should be better at fighting off colds and flu. Whether this response would endure after additional hours of sleep deprivation is not known, he said. And what it means to the brain is also not known.

Dr. James Krueger, a physiologist at the University of Tennessee in Memphis, and pioneer in the field of sleep and the immune system, has distilled his observations into a theory of sleep. The brain is composed of myriad groups of neutrons that carry out specific functions, he said. But during the day, not every group is called into play. If the neuronal groups are not stimulated, their connections may be lost. During sleep, Krueger said, the brain releases cytokines that induce a special firing pattern among various neuronal groups, preserving their connections for future use.

Thus, parts of the brain sleep while other parts are awake, Krueger said. The collective output of many such groups leads to what scientists called non-REM sleep, when dreams do not occur.

Such research has major implications for human ailments. Chronic fatigue syndrome could be related to the abnormal arousal of cytokines in the brain. Cancer patients and transplant patients are prone to developing bacterial infections of the blood similar to those seen in the sleep-deprived rats.

Sleep Deprivation Research

With a partner, prepare a report on the consequences of sleep deprivation by following the steps below.

1. Referring to the material from this unit, prepare a series of interview questions to use in a survey about sleep habits and sleep deprivation.

     First, discuss with your partner the results that you think your survey will give you. Based on your reading and discussions in class, what do you expect to discover about sleep habits and the consequences of sleep deprivation?

     Think about what questions you need to ask people to check your predictions about their habits and sleep deprivation.

     Create questions that will give you information you can easily tabulate or record to get numbers. The most useful kinds for this survey are closed questions and Likert Scale questions.

   a) A **closed question** is a question that asks for a yes, no, or one-word answer.

     Example: Do you feel angry if you get little sleep?   yes___ no___

   b) A **Likert Scale** (from 1 to 5) is a type of survey question that provides easily tabulated results.

     Example: Rate your mood after getting little sleep.

     1 (very irritable)
     2 (somewhat irritable)
     3 (neither irritable nor cheerful)
     4 (somewhat cheerful)
     5 (very cheerful)

     Write the questions on a separate sheet of paper, leaving plenty of space after each to record the answers.

2. Test your questions out on classmates to be sure that your survey will provide you with the information you need.

3. Conduct your survey. **Be sure to record all the answers.**

4. List your results on a separate sheet of paper.

5. Write a report on your research. Divide it into four sections: introduction, method, results, and discussion.

   • For the **introduction**, give background information about the consequences of sleep deprivation and explain what you were trying to discover in this survey.

   • For the **method** section, describe the population (the people you surveyed) in terms of gender, culture, and other relevant characteristics. How long have they been here? What questions did you ask them? List the questions and explain the reason for asking each one.

   • For the **results** section, show the statistical results of your survey. Provide tables or charts.

   • For the **discussion** section, explain what the results mean and relate them to the background information and purpose that you described in the introduction. Was your survey successful? What do the results tell us?

6. Exchange reports with another pair, and discuss the similarites and differences. Focus on these components: the introduction, the questions, the results of the survey, and the conclusion.

7 Aging: Can We All Live to Be Over 100 Years Old?

This unit focuses on aging and longevity, or living to be very old. It involves reading about the factors that influence how long people live. It also gives scientific information about how the process of aging happens, and some ideas about how to slow the aging process. The unit leads to a lot of discussion as you share stories and information from the reading.

The final task in this unit is to write a short essay about the topic. To prepare, you will try to organize the information from the unit in an academic way to create a convincing argument.

You should turn to the project description at the end of the unit regularly to see how much information and how many skills you need to help you complete it.

READING *You will read for information, and skim and scan academic text to get the most important information for your purposes.*

LISTENING *You will listen to a lecture to identify possible solutions to a problem and explain how they work.*

WRITING *You will write short answers to tasks presented in the unit. You will write a full, brief academic essay in a step-by-step way, collaborating with classmates.*

SPEAKING *You will discuss your opinions and information presented in the unit. You will talk and work together to write the final essay, giving advice and asking questions about other people's work.*

TO BEGIN, TURN THE PAGE AND START THINKING ABOUT AND DISCUSSING THE TOPIC IN GENERAL.

Introduction to the Topic

● SHARING PERSONAL AND BACKGROUND INFORMATION
● PREDICTING

1. Answer the following three questions on your own, and then form a group of three people to share your information.

   a) Who is the oldest person you know or have heard about?

   _____

   b) How did that person live to be so old? Why did she or he outlive other people?

   _____

   _____

   _____

   _____

   c) What are some factors that enable people to live to be very old?

   _____

   _____

   _____

   _____

2. Share your information with the class. On the blackboard, list the factors you have discussed. Can you find some common patterns in the lists you have created?

3. Now answer the following questions on your own. When you are finished, share your answers with the class.

   a) Would you like to live to be extremely old?

   _____

   b) If you could live to be extremely old by changing your lifestyle, would you try to do it?

   _____

   c) If you could live to be extremely old by taking medication, would you do so?

   _____

4. Compare your answers to these questions with those of the rest of the class. Does the class generally agree on these issues?

TASK 2

Getting a General Idea from Examples

● GETTING THE MAIN IDEA FROM DESCRIPTION
● SUMMARIZING

Do **either** activity 1 **or** activity 2 below. Share the information in the reading and your list with someone else in the class who has read the other text.

1. The first text is a short newspaper article. Read about **Campodimele, Italy**, an area of the world where people generally live to be extremely old.

   In the space below, list the factors that have enabled the people of Campodimele to live so long.

2. The second text is taken from an anthropology textbook. Read about **Abkhasia**, an area of the world in which people generally live to be extremely old. Abkhasia is a region of what is now the Republic of Georgia.

   In the space below, list the factors that have enabled the people of Abkhasia to live so long.

3. As a class, compare the lists of factors you created above with the list of factors you created in Task 1. Are there many similarities? Are there many differences?

VILLAGERS LIVE LONG ON VEGGIES, NO STRESS

BY CLAUDIA PARSONS

REUTER

CAMPODIMELE, Italy—The inhabitants of this medieval village may well have found the recipe for a long and healthy life—lots of vegetables and no stress.

Campodimele sits on a rocky hilltop some 150 kilometres south of Rome. The fortified wall that surrounds the traffic-free centre—a maze of narrow alleys, stairways and piazzas—dates from the 14th century, when the village was a retreat from bandits on the plain below.

The legacy of this checkered past is a sedate one.

Today, the village, whose name translates as "field of honey," is best known for the longevity of its 850 residents.

Mayor Paolo Zannella says it's rare for anyone to die before age 85 and 40 percent of the population is older than 80. The average life span of an Italian man is 73, while women tend to live into their early 80s.

"But what is unusual," said Paolo's brother, Pietro, "is that Campodimelans don't just grow old, they stay healthy as well.

"There is a woman who had her 99th birthday a few days ago who is completely self-sufficient. Her son wanted her to go and live with him in the city, but she said she would rather live on her own here.

"She's been using a stick (cane) for a year now," he joked, "but in my opinion it's just to show she's old, rather than because she needs it."

In 1985, World Health Organization researchers discovered cholesterol levels in 80-year-old Campodimelans lower than in new-born babies.

More recently, Prof. Pietro Cugini of Rome's Policlinico hospital spent two months looking at 92 villagers between the ages of 76 and 102. He found blood pressure substantially lower than the national average.

"Their lifestyle is beautifully structured," he said. "They get up at dawn and go to bed early, and eat at the same time every day.

"They are wonderfully synchronized with their natural biological rhythms."

Campodimelans—whose diet is based on fresh vegetables, supplemented by snails and wild mushrooms—were equally keen to relate their longevity and good health to their way of life.

Zannella, the middle-aged mayor, said: "If I had to list the ingredients of our elixir of life, I would put in first place the easy temper and calm of the villagers.

"Everyone has a sense of balance and equilibrium. The word 'stress' is practically unknown."

Reprinted with permission of Reuters.

ABKHASIA

The first cry of the normal newborn in Philadelphia or Conakry, in Moscow or Shanghai, has the same pitch and key. Each essentially says, "I am here! I am a member of your family and group." In all societies, babies arrive, suckle, and grow into restless and questioning youth. As adults they mate, toil, quarrel, seek, and hope (Sandburg, 1956). Ultimately, they too die. In sum, life is always an unfinished business, and death is its only cessation (Montagu, 1981).

Although you use chronological age as a convenient marker, the meaning of this dimension is a social one, with vast consequences for health, longevity, happiness, and well-being. This fact is highlighted by the inhabitants of Abkhasia, a small, mountainous Soviet republic wedged between the Black Sea and the High Caucasus. The Abkhasians are a tall, slender, narrow-faced, fair-skinned people. Older men develop bushy eyebrows which, together with their luxuriant mustaches, give them a dignified, stern demeanor. The women are a bit shorter than the men, graceful, with high foreheads and long, slender necks. A 1979 Soviet census found 548 Abkhasians, out of a population of 520,000, who claimed to be 100 years of age or older. When the cases were investigated, the number of centenarians was pared to 241—in proportion, a figure still five times higher than that of the United States (Sullivan, 1982).

Medical researchers are uniformly impressed by the alertness, excellent muscle tone, and mental and physical capabilities of Abkhasians of all ages. Consider Khfaf Lasuria, who at age 113 joined a troupe of thirty dancers, each of whom is 90 years of age or older. An able dancer, she was still performing happily before audiences when she was 131 years old. Not too far from her lived Akhutsa Kunach, age 114. While he was cutting timber in the woods, a tree fell on him and broke three of his ribs. Two months later, recovered, he had resumed forestry (Benet, 1974).

Social and cultural factors contribute to the long lives of the Abkhasians. Age is an honored and esteemed status, one that takes precedence over wealth and social position. Those of advanced age participate in the council of elders and are regularly sought out by the young. The elderly do not retire, but continue to work until they die, so at no stage of life does an Abkhasian become sedentary. Moreover, Abkhasian diets coincide with practices nutritionists define as ideal. And strong kinship ties pervade and regulate interpersonal relationships. The high degree of social integration and continuity that characterizes their personal lives allows the Abkhasians to adapt to changing circumstances at a comfortable pace. Although they have not discovered the fountain of youth, the people of Abkhasia seem to have developed the next best thing—an involved old age.

James W. VanderZanden, *The Social Experience: An Introduction to Sociology.* © 1988. Reproduced with permission of The McGraw-Hill Companies.

TASK 3

Getting Specific Information About the Topic

- READING FOR COMPLETE UNDERSTANDING
- RELATING READ INFORMATION TO PREVIOUS INFORMATION

OXYGEN

1. Read the title and subtitle of the following newspaper article. What do you expect to learn from reading this text?

   _____

   _____

2. Read the first and last sentences of the article. Do they confirm what you predicted in question 1 above?

   _____

3. Now read the first section of the text and answer the questions below.

   a) What is a free radical?

   _____

   _____

   b) How much of the ingested oxygen becomes free radicals?

   _____

   c) How do free radicals cause aging?

   _____

   _____

   _____

4. Now read the rest of the article to answer the questions below.

   a) Besides oxygen, where do free radicals come from?

   _____

   _____

   b) Why don't vitamins help us to avoid the problem of free radicals?

   _____

   _____

c) What is the problem with exercise?

_____

_____

_____

d) What seems to be the only way to reduce free radicals?

_____

_____

_____

5. How does this information relate to the information you have read about longevity in Campodimele and Abkhasia?

_____

_____

_____

_____

READING **OXYGEN**

Its spent waste causes our living cells to age

REUTER

SAN ANTONIO, TEX.

Oxygen gives life, but it also may help take it away.

"Oxygen is both a blessing and curse," says physiologist Byung Pal Yu. "We must have oxygen to survive, but it is also a source of damage to cellular functions."

Yu, who is researching the aging process at the University of Texas Health Science Centre in San Antonio, said experiments indicate that oxygen causes living cells to age because of the effects of respiratory waste products called "free radicals."

He said in an interview that most of the oxygen humans breathe combines with hydrogen and converts into water, which is excreted from the body in several ways. However, as much as eight percent of the oxygen taken in converts into unstable "free radicals."

Those free radicals then career through the body, modifying healthy cells they come in contact with, Yu said.

When a free radical pairs up with a fat cell, for example, the fat cell is converted into the harmful chemical hydrogen peroxide, he said.

"Over time, tissue is damaged by free radicals and that is what causes aging," said Yu.

Increasingly, free radical activity also is being looked at as a source of diseases such as cancer, diabetes, arteriosclerosis and arthritis, Yu said.

Aging theories associated with free radicals first emerged in the 1950s, but faded into obscurity, Yu said. Now, scientists are again focusing on the role of the unusual molecules in human health.

"Medicine is filled with fads. This is the latest one, but it appears to have some validity."

In addition to oxygen, free radicals come from sources such as X-rays, sunlight and hydrocarbons, Yu said. In effect, the human body is constantly bombarded by free radicals.

Humans survive this onslaught because the body has defence mechanisms that protect it from the effects of free radicals.

Vitamins E, C, and A, for example, absorb the pesky molecules and render them harmless. But, Yu said, "this defence system is not perfect so there is a continuous escape of free radicals."

However, he said there is no evidence that taking supplemental doses of the vitamins will make one immune from free radical effects.

"People have tried to slow down free radicals by taking lots of vitamins, but none of these chemicals have ever worked or had any beneficial effect in slowing down aging."

The problem, he said, is that vitamins cannot be distributed through the body in a way that they can capture enough free radicals to slow down aging.

Yu said his research also questions the theory that exercise is beneficial to humans. Exercise, he pointed out, increases the consumption of oxygen, which in turn leads to the formation of more free radicals.

There are studies now that indicate that some tissue in heart muscle "is shown to be damaged by strenuous exercise" that may actually be the result of free radical activity, he said.

Yu said the only effective means of reducing free radicals is to cut food intake. For reasons not completely understood, reduction of food somehow suppresses free radical reation, he said.

This may explain why experiments at the San Antonio centre show that rats live longer when their food consumption is cut, he said.

Yu does not hold out much hope that the effects of free radicals can be ameliorated enough to slow or stop the human aging process.

"About the only thing we can say is: Don't eat so much."

But in the long run, he added, given the necessity of oxygen to life, "We are doomed to die."

Reprinted with permission of Reuters.

TASK 4

More Specific Information

- READING FOR COMPLETE INFORMATION
- GETTING THE MAIN IDEA
- SUMMARIZING

THE DOWNSIDE OF BREATHING

1. Read these questions first, and then explore the following newspaper article to find the answers.

   a) What is "the ultimate paradox"?

   _____

   _____

   b) Name three substances that can protect humans from oxygen-related damage.

   _____

   _____

   _____

   c) What is an anti-oxidant?

   _____

   _____

   d) What concern does Brian Gillespie have?

   _____

   _____

2. Fill in the missing statements below to complete the process of how free radicals become dangerous.

   a) Free radicals search for electron mates

   b) _____

   c) Molecule has an electron imbalance

   d) _____

   e) It may cause cancer, cell damage, and genetic damage.

3. a) Divide the class into three groups. Each group will be responsible for one of the three anti-oxidants discussed in the reading. After reading and discussing your section, fill in the appropriate part of the table below.

   b) Now form new groups that consist of one member from each of the original groups. Together, try to complete the table by sharing your information about the three types of anti-oxidants orally. (Some boxes may have little or no information.)

   Try not to copy directly from the text. Your job is to get a general understanding of the reading, not to analyse every word.

	HEALTH BENEFITS	RESEARCH EVIDENCE	CONCERNS (IF ANY)
VITAMIN E			
VITAMIN C			
BETA-CAROTENE			

THE DOWNSIDE OF BREATHING

*Anti-oxidants may, or may not, save us from
that ultimate paradox—oxygen kills*

BY SHELLEY PAGE
Citizen science writer

We inhale oxygen thoughtlessly, indifferently, as though it were mere afterthought, just fribble. Or we take gulping greedy gasps of the life-giving gas, unable to get enough.

We are surrounded and suffused by oxygen. It enables us to live.

But there is a dark underbelly to oxygen. Just as it turns butter rancid and rusts car bodies, oxygen slowly destroys our organs, our cells, our DNA.

Breathing oxygen creates highly reactive molecules called free radicals that rampage through our bodies. Although essential to many metabolic reactions, an excess of these free radicals can make us old, cause cancers and heart disease. They're believed to aggravate or cause more than 60 afflictions linked to aging.

"This is the ultimate paradox: oxygen is essential for life yet we just wear out because of a constant reaction with oxygen," says Graham Burton, a senior researcher at the National Research Council. He is one of the researchers trying to tinker with our Faustian bargain with oxygen.

While rust-proofing protects cars and preservatives keep butter fresh, scientists believe there are substances that can protect humans from the ravages of oxygen. Vitamins E and C along with beta-carotene may act as anti-oxidants to help stop the ravages of free radicals. Anti-oxidants have been found in green tea, red wine and garlic.

These days we can't open a health magazine or turn on the television without hearing boasts that anti-oxidants neutralize these free radicals and prevent heart disease, cure cancer, even aging. Not even a snake oil salesman would make such claims.

"Three quarters of a million people die of a heart attack every year," says Harvard's Victor Rimm, who surveyed 40,000 men and found vitamin E reduces the risk of heart attack.

"If you want to wait 20 years (for more studies), that's a lot of people who will die," Rimm told a recent forum on anti-oxidants in the U.S.

Many longevity seekers are already hedging their bets by gobbling mouthfuls of these nutrients. A recent study of Canadians says vitamins C and E are our favorites.

But many scientists fear people think these cheap little pills, available at any drug store, are magic bullets. The world of anti-oxidants, researchers say, is unbelievably complex.

"I'm concerned about what's happening out there, we don't know enough to be taking these vitamins at high doses for long periods of time," says Brian Gillespie, chief of drug evaluation for non-prescription drugs at Health Canada. He's rejected requests from vitamin companies who want to put health claims on vitamin bottles.

There are many questions.

No one knows, for example, which anti-oxidants work on which diseases. No one knows if the anti-oxidants work alone or in consort. No one is clear about how they work. No one really knows what doses are useful or if taking too much can cause long-term harm.

While scientists work to answer these questions their best advice is: Eat lots of fruits and vegetables.

We couldn't wiggle our nose, recall a memory or screw the lid off a vitamin bottle without free radicals. They're essential to many metabolic reactions in the body. White blood cells, for example, produce free radicals in their chemical warfare against viruses.

But trouble starts when something upsets the body's biochemical balance and creates an excess of free radicals—unstable molecules lacking the normal complement of paired electrons.

"It's like a dangerous game of molecular tag," says Burton.

Free radicals cruise through our bodies searching for an electron mate. When they link up with another molecule, that molecule suddenly has an extra electron. To restore its electrical

Free Radical Damage to Living Cells

Damage to DNA

Free radicals

Damage to cell membrane

Damage to Mitochondria (the cell's power source)

balance, the molecule latches on to yet another molecule. This process triggers a toxic chain reaction that wreaks havoc in the body, possibly causing cancers. Cells are destroyed or damaged. Genes are chewed up or reprogrammed.

Free radicals can also attack the fat in our bodies, leading to heart disease.

The build-up in the arteries of cholesterol—the white, fatty substance used to make cell membranes—can cause heart disease. These fat globs are carried through the bloodstream aboard protein molecules known as low-density lipoprotein.

Free radicals can oxidize these lipoproteins, turning them "bad," just as butter goes rancid. The body's immune system sends in special white blood cells called macrophages to help unclog the mess. But macrophages get stuffed full of fat and stick inside the walls of the arteries. The build-up narrows arteries, sometimes blocking them, which leads to heart attack or stroke.

Our body has built-in protection against free radicals. Enzymes that neutralize them, mechanisms that repair damage. We also make ingenious use of natural anti-oxidants in our diet, like vitamins, which bond chemically with these radicals and slow down their wear and tear.

With age, and the ravages of smog and tobacco smoke, we can't keep free radicals in check as we used to.

Scientists think the body may need extra help: Anti-oxidant supplements.

Vitamin E

Seeds on the ground that are waiting to germinate protect themselves with an outer shell made of vitamin E. It bonds with the free radicals of oxygen so they can't destroy the seed's shell.

"Animals evolved, they ate vitamin E, they used this molecule to protect their own membranes from the radicals," says Keith Ingold, an NRC expert in protecting oils, metals and humans from free radicals.

We already use vitamin E to protect ourselves from oxygen. There is special hope that taking supplements will prevent heart disease.

Recent research has shown:

• Studies of 120,000 people in the United States showed big amounts of vitamin E seem to significantly cut the risk of heart disease. Studies of more than 80,000 female nurses and 40,000 male health-care professionals found an association—although not a causal link—between taking as much as 14 times the daily recommended allowance of vitamin E for at least two years and a reduced risk of heart disease—by almost one half for women, one-third for men.

• A study of nearly 30,000 residents of an area of north-central China where cancer death rates are among the world's highest showed that those taking supplements of beta-carotene, vitamin E and selenium, all believed to be anti-oxidants, saw their overall cancer death rate drop by 13 percent and the risk of death from all causes decrease by nine percent. Researchers from the National Cancer Institute in the U.S. said this was the first evidence from an extensive human study that vitamin supplements reduced the risk of cancer.

But there are problems with the studies.

Health professionals may be more health conscious, leading to better health. And researchers don't know the long-term effects of taking supplements. McMaster University researchers recently announced they're putting vitamin E to its stiffest test yet.

Over the next four years they'll follow 6,000 men and 3,000 women over the age of 55, comparing how they do on 400 international units (IUs) of vitamin E, a high blood pressure medication, both or a placebo. They'll see how many have heart attacks or strokes.

It's difficult to get large amounts of vitamin E from our diet. It's found in vegetable oil, wheat germ, egg yolk and leafy vegetables. So you'd have to take supplements to get the large doses—more than 100 IUs—used in the studies.

The doses of vitamin E people took in the heart disease studies were many times larger than the recommended daily dose in Canada, which is nine milligrams for men, six for women.

Gillespie, of Health Canada, says there have been reports that doses of between 400 and 800 IUs may cause blurred vision, breast enlargement, diarrhea, flu-like symptoms or tiredness and weakness. Larger doses could cause increased bleeding in people with a vitamin K deficiency.

Vitamin C

Nobel-prize winning chemist Linus Pauling was denounced as a crank when he started gobbling mega-doses of vitamin C a few decades ago. Now, it's the vitamin of choice among Canadians surveyed.

But researchers still debate Pauling's claims that the vitamin has medicinal abilities ranging from curing the common cold to cancer.

For example, the two studies that found benefits to taking vitamin E surprisingly found no benefits from taking vitamin C in either heart disease or cancer.

"Clearly we don't know what's going on here. Vitamin E and C are both anti-oxidants," says Gillespie.

There is some evidence vitamin C works as an anti-oxidant preventing stomach cancer, where it sponges up nitrosomines—carcinogens found in our bodies but also in meats, cheeses and other foods cured with nitrites.

Although there are few studies showing conclusive benefits, Burton says if you withdraw vitamin C from the diet, "you get striking physiological symptoms. Teeth fall out, humans can die."

In Canada, the recommended dose for men is 40 mg a day. For women it's 30 mg. That's very low compared to the megadoses some people are taking.

Experts say there's no evidence taking mega-doses will harm people, unless they have an iron deficiency. Again, most researchers say more studies are needed.

Beta-Carotene

For several years we've been told to eat our carrots and squash to get the benefits of the anti-oxidant beta-carotene. We've been told it will protect us from many cancers, especially lung cancer.

But Canadian research is questioning this "assumption."

"I feel there has been an unquestioning acceptance of carotene being an anti-oxidant with no real proof of how it might work," says Burton.

He thinks beta-carotene might actually work in the opposite way many researchers assumed.

"Perhaps it reacts very readily with oxygen, producing many compounds we don't yet understand."

He is working with biologist Jenny Phipps at the NRC to see how the many derivatives of beta-carotene work.

Phipps is introducing a beta-carotene derivative called retinoic acid, a form of vitamin A, to a wide variety of cancer cells to see if she can stop their proliferation. She's searching for a less toxic cancer treatment.

This doesn't mean beta-carotene doesn't prevent cancer. It may mean we can't be too quick to assume that free radicals are all bad and anti-oxidants are all good.

Beta-carotene, converted to vitamin A by the body, has been hotly pursued because it may have the protective properties of vitamin A without its toxic side-effects, which include liver damage at high doses.

Because it isn't a vitamin there's no daily recommended dose for beta-carotene. If you want to play it safe, eat fruits and vegetables.

And that's still the best advice for the health conscious.

"Take everything in moderation," says Burton, who admits to taking vitamin E supplements when he remembers.

TASK 5

Testing Ability to Get Specific Information About the Topic

● READING FOR COMPLETE UNDERSTANDING

Answer the questions below while reading this newspaper article. Read the questions first, and then scan the text for answers.

You have 20 minutes to finish. Check your score out of 14 points after discussing the answers as a class.

1. What is one of biology's basic mysteries? (1 point)

   _____

2. What substances cause our decline and eventual death? (1 point)

   _____

3. How are free radicals created? (2 points)

   _____

4. Where are mitochondria? (1 point)

   _____

5. How does a free radical differ from a regular oxygen molecule? (1 point)

   _____

6. Name one reason why humans age more slowly than some other animals. (1 point)

   _____

7. Match these pieces of information according to the information in the text. (4 points)

   a) DNA in nucleus
   b) Mitochondrial DNA

   ___ suffers more free radical damage

   ___ is the location where free radicals are made

   ___ has a repair system

   ___ is the location where free radical damage is permanent

8. What do cells use to fight back against free radicals? (1 point)

   _____

9. Why is manganese SOD important? (2 points)

   _____

   _____

A DIP IN THE FOUNTAIN OF YOUTH

Scientists are working hard to make growing old obsolete—or at the very least alter the aging process to extend life and health

BY JUDY FOREMAN
Boston Globe

In Oklahoma and Kentucky, a chemical has reversed brain damage in aging gerbils. In Baltimore, the same chemical has extended the lifespan of mice by 20 percent, the equivalent of giving 15 more years to 75-year-old humans.

In Utah, another drug has rejuvenated the failing immune systems of aged rats so quickly—within 24 hours—that AIDS patients now scramble for street versions of it.

In Milwaukee and North Chicago, scientists have rolled back the physiological clock for older men taking injections of growth hormone. This fall, a handful of Americans will become guinea pigs for yet another drug with Fountain of Youth potential.

Throughout the country—and, indeed, the world—scientists are concocting drugs and tinkering with genes in a race to unravel one of biology's most basic mysteries: aging.

Their grandest hope is to make aging obsolete. But even reaching a more modest goal would be reward enough, altering the basic mechanisms of aging enough to extend life and health.

Now, for the first time, the tools are at hand.

So far, there is no all-encompassing theory of aging and, hence, no one drug likely to block all facets of the aging process. But once-disparate pieces of the aging puzzle are coming together. The very basic biological mechanisms, at last, are beginning to be understood.

Perhaps the most basic of those is a theory that what eventually causes our decline is the tremendous wreckage to cell membranes, proteins and even our genes by toxic forms of oxygen called free radicals.

Free radical molecules, among the most highly reactive chemicals on Earth, are spewed out by the billions in the body every day in the normal course of burning food with oxygen to make energy.

This combustion takes place in "little fireplaces" within the cell called mitochondria, says Douglas Wallace, a geneticist at Emory University in Atlanta. In the process, some electrons wind up on oxygen molecules, turning them into dangerous free radicals.

The first glimmerings of the extent of free radical damage came a few years ago, when California biochemist Bruce Ames showed that free radicals in animals destroy DNA in the very heart of a cell, its nucleus, at an enormous rate and that this damage increases with age.

In rats, free radicals damage 50,000 tiny bits of DNA every day in every cell, says Ames, head of the National Institute of Environmental Health Sciences Center at the University of California-Berkeley. Because debris from this damage shows up in urine, Ames is developing a urine test that could someday be used as a measure of aging.

In young animals, much of the damage is repaired by special DNA enzymes that cruise along looking for unnatural twists and breaks in DNA. But over time, the DNA repair system cannot keep up, and the damage accumulates. Eventually, Ames says, an old rat can end up with "two million lesions or damaged sites in DNA per cell."

In humans, who breathe oxygen at a much lower rate, the damage rate is lower, although still deadly, Ames adds.

But even more important than free radical damage to DNA in the nucleus, researchers have found in the past year, is damage to DNA in the mitochondria, whose daily output of energy is essential to maintain life.

Free radical damage to mitochondrial DNA now appears to be so profound—it suffers 10 times more damage than DNA in the nucleus—that it "may be the major element that ties all the other theories of aging together," Wallace says.

For one thing, free radicals are made inside mitochondria, making DNA there an easy target. For another, mitochondrial DNA, unlike DNA in the nucleus, has little or no repair system. Once damage occurs, it is likely to be permanent. Damage to mitochondrial DNA accumulates so steadily that scientists now use it as an "aging clock."

Although it takes three decades before mitochondrial damage becomes serious in humans, Wallace says, free radicals begin to "knock out so much mitochondrial DNA" after age 30 that energy production falls. Over time, it becomes inadequate to maintain health and life.

Cells fight back with the ancient defences—antioxidant enzymes developed by Earth's earliest cells to detoxify dangerous forms of oxygen. In fact, the reason humans live longer than most other species is that we have unusually high levels of a particular antioxidant, manganese SOD, that protects mitochondria, says Richard Cutler, a biophysicist at the National Institute on Aging (NIA).

But over time, says Earl Stadtman, biochemistry chief of the National Heart, Lung and Blood Institute, the wreckage piles up.

TASK 6

Listening for Solutions

● GUIDED NOTETAKING

The lecture you will listen to discusses six possible ways to fight aging. While listening, fill in the information below. (Some answers have been provided.) When you have finished, compare notes with a partner and the teacher.

1. a) First way to fight aging:

   _____

   _____

   _____

   b) How it works:

   _____

   _____

   _____

   _____

2. a) Second way to fight aging:

   _____

   _____

   _____

   b) How it works:

   _____

   _____

   _____

   _____

3. a) Third way to fight aging:

   _____

   _____

   _____

   b) How it works:

   _____

   _____

   _____

   _____

4. a) Fourth way to fight aging:

_____

_____

_____

b) How it works:

_____

_____

_____

_____

5. a) Fifth way to fight aging: **Deprenyl**
   b) How it works: **increases levels of dopamine, which blocks creation of free radicals**

6. a) Sixth way to fight aging: **human growth hormone**
   b) How it works:

_____

_____

_____

_____

_____

TASK 7

Checking Knowledge of Vocabulary

● DEFINING TERMS

1. Divide the class into two equal-sized teams. One team will receive **Vocabulary List A**, and the other will receive **Vocabulary List B**. (Your teacher will provide you with these lists.)

2. In your group, study the list of words from the unit and be sure you understand what the terms mean and how to explain them.

3. Join with one partner from the other group. Take turns explaining one word from your list **without actually saying it or giving hints about spelling**. Your partner will then guess which term you are explaining. Go through your lists in this way word by word and count the number of correct guesses you make. The pair with the highest score is the winner.

Essay

Your final assignment for this unit on aging is to write an essay responding to the following statement:

It is possible for most people to live to be more than 100 years old.

The following steps will help you to prepare.

1. To begin, take a look at the list of factors influencing longevity that you prepared in Tasks 1 and 2. As well, review the scientific evidence relating to free radicals and anti-oxidants. You may wish to include some information on other ways of fighting aging from the reading in Task 5 and the lecture in Task 6.

2. With a partner, go through your notes and answers from the unit. Decide which information is **most useful** for your essay.

3. List your points on a separate piece of paper. Discuss them with a partner. Focus on how to **organize** the information effectively.

   Here are some suggestions to help you write a convincing academic argument:

   • Decide whether you **agree or disagree** with the statement.

   • In the **introduction**, start with a **thesis statement**, and then list the factors you will discuss to prove your thesis.

   • Make each paragraph of the body of the essay a discussion of **one** factor. Start these paragraphs with a topic sentence introducing the factor. Then, describe how the factor affects longevity. Avoid relying too heavily on stories and examples—**explain** it, do not just describe it.

   • Write a brief **conclusion** restating your thesis and pointing out how you proved it. List the factors again in the conclusion.

4. At each step of the writing process, discuss your writing with a classmate or two. These discussions can help you to focus and improve the essay. If your partners do not understand what you have written, you may need to revise the writing in some parts.

5. **Edit** the essay for grammar and vocabulary problems only after you have finished organizing it and clarifying the points you have made. Check particular language problems with the teacher.

6. **Evaluate** your work when you feel you have finished. Use the following questions to help you decide how well you did.

   a) What are the strengths of the essay?

   b) What are the weak parts, or what would you change if you could?

c) What type of feedback do you want from the teacher?

d) Do you feel that the essay is really responding to the statement?

e) Does the essay have a clearly stated thesis?

f) Have you listed the factors at the beginning?

g) Does each paragraph have a topic sentence?

h) Does each paragraph explain the factor being discussed?

i) Is the conclusion a good restatement of the thesis, and does it list the factors again?

8 Altruism: Why Don't We Always Help?

This unit focuses on altruism and prosocial behaviour, or helping people in an emergency. It involves reading about the factors that influence whether or not and why people help. It also leads to a lot of discussion as you share stories and complex information from the reading.

The final project in this unit is to write a short essay about the topic. To prepare, you will try to organize the information from the unit in an academic way to create a convincing argument.

You should turn to the project description at the end of the unit regularly to see how much information and how many skills you need to help you complete it.

READING   *You will read for complete information, and skim and scan academic text to get the most important information for your purposes. All reading will be collaborative and interactive.*

LISTENING   *You will listen to a brief lecture summarizing points about the topic.*

WRITING   *You will write short answers to tasks presented in the unit. You will write a full, brief academic essay in a step-by-step way, collaborating with classmates.*

SPEAKING   *You will discuss your opinions, tell stories, and share information presented in the unit. You will talk and work together to write the final essay, giving advice and asking questions about other people's writing.*

TO BEGIN, TURN THE PAGE AND START THINKING ABOUT AND DISCUSSING THE TOPIC IN GENERAL.

Introduction to the Topic

● DISCUSSING PERSONAL
INFORMATION, BACKGROUND
INFORMATION, IDEAS

THINKING ABOUT ALTRUISM: DEFINITIONS

1. Look in an English-English dictionary for the word
altruism. Working with a partner, define altruism in
your own words:

_____

_____

_____

_____

2. Make a list of words related to altruism, either negative or
positive.

3. Without using words, illustrate the meaning of altruism.
Use symbols and images.

4. Share your definition, list, and illustration with another
pair.
a) What do your ideas have in common?

_____

_____

_____

_____

b) How are they different?

_____

_____

_____

_____

Sharing Experiences About the Topic

- NARRATING
- PREDICTING

THINKING ABOUT ALTRUISM: EXPERIENCES

1. Think about a story of altruism that you know, either from your life or from something you have heard or read. Prepare to tell it to a partner. Use the space below to make notes to get ready.

2. Compare your story with a partner's. Do your stories share anything in common? If so, what? Write your answer below.

   _____

   _____

3. In a group of three people, discuss what factors influence whether one person will help another in an emergency such as a fire, an accident, or a crime. List the factors here:

Reading Examples to Illustrate the Topic

- READING NARRATIVE
- SUMMARIZING
- PREDICTING

REAL-LIFE HORROR STORIES

The following reading is from a social psychology textbook. Working with a partner, follow the instructions below.

1. Read the three stories as quickly as possible.

2. Retell the stories to each other to be sure that you under-stand them.

3. What do the stories have in common? Write your answer below.

   _____

   _____

   _____

4. What could have caused the people to behave as they did? Write your answer below.

_____

_____

_____

5. Share your answer to question 4 with the rest of the class. List all the possibilities on the blackboard.

6. Now discuss this statement as a class: **People will only help others in certain situations.** Write notes from the discussion here:

READING

REAL-LIFE HORROR STORIES

Some people devote themselves to selfless service to others. Mother Teresa, a Roman Catholic nun, has chosen to dedicate her life to the orphaned, the sick, and the poor in the slums of Calcutta. Norman Bethune gave up a life of luxury to provide medical support for foreign armies fighting for causes which he believed to be in the best interests of humanity. More recently, in 1992 31-year-old Eric Hoskins was awarded the Pearson Peace Medal in recognition of five years of extraordinary effort to provide humanitarian assistance to children in Iraq, Somalia, and Sudan—countries ravaged by war.

People like Norman Bethune, Mother Teresa, and Eric Hoskins stand as testimony to the human willingness to sacrifice comfort, security, and prestige in order to help other less fortunate people. Sadly, the human story has its darker side: not only do most people *not* live up to these models of selflessness, but even worse, they often fail to assist people in urgent need of help, even when doing so might simply involve telephoning an ambulance or the police.

For example, in 1985, a man who tried to stop a group of teenagers who had stolen candy from a counter in the Toronto subway was savagely beaten while more than a hundred people looked on and did nothing; no one even called for help (*The Toronto Star*, January 19, 1985). In 1978, a dozen or more people refused to help a father rescue his seven-year-old son who had fallen into the Rivière des Prairies near Montreal. As they watched the boy drown, one person was heard to say "We're not going in there—the water's too dirty," referring to the fact that the boy had fallen in close to a sewage outlet (*The Globe and Mail*, January 6, 1978). In the same year in Edmonton, a 22-year-old woman stepped off a bus on her way home from work one night, unaware that a man on the bus had got off just behind her. A short distance from the bus stop, he assaulted her, beating her in the face, stripping off her clothing, and then raping her. Wearing only a coat, with blood flowing from her eyes, she sought help in a nearby apartment where she was told by a tenant to get out. She ran out to the street and asked two passersby for help, and was told to go to a nearby pay telephone. Finally, she found help at an all-night grocery where the staff called the police (*The Toronto Star*, November 1, 1978).

A Textbook of Social Psychology, Third Edition, J. E. Alcock, D. W. Carment, S. W. Sadava, © 1994. Used by permission of Prentice Hall Canada Inc.

● PREDICTING
● GETTING THE MAIN IDEA
● SUMMARIZING

Getting Specific Information About the Topic

FACTORS WHICH INFLUENCE PROSOCIAL BEHAVIOUR

1. Before reading the following academic text, take some time in a group of five to discuss the influence that each of the factors below might have on prosocial behaviour. Write a few notes on each factor in the table.

FACTOR	POSSIBLE INFLUENCE
CULTURAL DIFFERENCES	
PERSONALITY VARIABLES	
GENDER DIFFERENCES	
EFFECTS OF RELIGION	
RURAL-URBAN DIFFERENCES	

2. Now divide the five sections of the reading among you. Read your section of the text, and fill in the appropriate boxes in the second and third columns of the table below. In the fourth column, enter *yes*, *no*, or *partly* to show whether or not the reading confirms your prediction.

    Remember that your job here is to get a general idea of the information. Do not copy from the text.

3. After filling in your boxes of the table, discuss the information with a classmate who has read the same section of the text. Compare your notes.

4. Return to your original group and help each other to complete the table by telling each other about what you have read. You will need this information to complete the unit's final project. Follow these guidelines:

    • Do not refer back to the text during this discussion.

    • Do not show your notes to the other group members.

    • Do not read aloud from your notes.

	EFFECT	RESEARCH	PREDICTION CONFIRMED?
CULTURAL DIFFERENCES			
PERSONALITY VARIABLES			
GENDER DIFFERENCES			
EFFECTS OF RELIGION			
RURAL-URBAN DIFFERENCES			

5. Go back to your original predictions. As a class, discuss the differences between your predictions and the information in the reading.

FACTORS WHICH INFLUENCE PROSOCIAL BEHAVIOUR

Cultural differences

There are great differences in when and how concern is shown for others among the many cultures of the world. Unfortunately, perhaps because of the inherent methodological difficulties, few psychological studies of altruism have been conducted cross-culturally. Anthropological research suggests that the emphasis put on altruism in Western societies is relatively rare in other parts of the world (Cohen, 1972) and appears to be the product of a love-oriented parent-child relationship and stable, monogamous marriages. The latter may be in the process of waning and, as the family becomes less and less effective as a socializer of children in North American society, we may be in danger of producing a generation of undersocialized children (Rushton, 1980).

Of the few studies that have been conducted, some have found subjects in the United States to be less willing to provide help; others have found the opposite. In research which compared the prosocial behaviour of children in India, Kenya, Mexico, the Philippines, Japan, and the United States, children in the United States were the *least* helpful in terms of offering assistance or advice to others in distress (Whiting and Whiting, 1975). The authors of that study concluded that prosocial behaviour is most evident among children who grow up in cultures where it is required of them—for example, in societies in which the typical family size is large and the child is required to share in the care and raising of other children and in managing the household.

Personality variables

As with any other behaviour, individuals differ in the degree to which they exhibit prosocial behaviour even though they have shared a common environment. Naturally, social psychologists have attempted to find personality correlates of altruism but the studies that have been done are not conclusive. For example, subjects who help have been found to be more socially oriented and more "internal" in terms of locus-of-control than subjects who do not help (Krebs, 1970; Ubbink and Sadava, 1974).

Although some researchers feel that it is futile to seek general personality predictors of helping behaviour (e.g., Gergen, Gergen and Meter, 1972), Rushton (1980, 1984) believes that the evidence is substantial enough to support the concept of a broadly-based altruistic trait. He argues that there is an "altruistic personality," which is associated with higher internalized standards of justice and responsibility, and with greater empathy, self-control, and integrity. However, much more evidence is required before the existence of such a personality pattern can be considered demonstrable. In any case, the way in which a particular personality trait is manifested is likely to vary with the situational context (Carlo, Eisenberg, Troyer, Switzer and Speer, 1991), so that an individual who acts prosocially in some situations (e.g., making donations to the United Appeal) may not do so in others (e.g., helping a drunk across a busy street).

Gender differences

As we have seen, empathy may play an important role in prosocial behaviour. There are, of course, individual differences in empathy, just as there are differences in the extent to which various situations elicit empathy (Archer *et al.*, 1981). There may also be differences in empathy resulting from gender roles. Since women have been found to experience more vicarious affective responses than men, perhaps because men have been trained traditionally to suppress emotional displays (Hoffman, 1977), we might expect women to be more empathic. Yet, taking the evidence as a whole, it is not clear whether or not genuine gender differences in empathy exist; females *do* describe themselves as being more empathic than do males, but this may reflect more the image that is expected of them rather than some predisposition (Eisenberg and Lennon, 1983). Nor is there any clear evidence about gender differences in the willingness to help others, although adult women appear to be more willing to help highly dependent people, while men appear more helpful to those who are not so dependent (Schopler and Bateson, 1965). This could reflect the "caring" role which many females are brought up to assume.

The traditional norms which govern helping are quite different for males and females in our society (Eagly and Crowley, 1986; Eagly, 1987). Males are expected both to rescue others who are in difficulty and to demonstrate courtesy and protectiveness towards subordinates. Such behaviour is expected both in close relationships and among strangers. Women, on the other hand, are expected to help through caring and nurturing other people, especially those within a close relationship. Women are actively discouraged from associating with strangers; this prohibition most likely discourages women from giving help to strangers as well.

In general, the research on helping behaviour suggests that men help more often than women, although there is a great deal of inconsistency in this regard from one study to another. It must also be remembered, however, that social psychological research has typically focused on short-term interactions with strangers and has therefore excluded by and large the very behaviours which are prescribed for the female gender role—behaviours which are manifest primarily in close, long-term relationships (Eagly and Crowley, 1986). Furthermore, since men and women still tend to occupy different social and occupational roles, the "masculine" roles and the skills that are acquired in them may better prepare men to assist others in distress. As women begin to assume traditional male roles, the differences in helping between the two sexes, even in the short-term interactions of the laboratory, may begin to disappear.

Effects of religion

We naturally wonder about the effects of being religious on the propensity to be helpful. After all, Christianity, Judaism, Islam, Hinduism and Buddhism all promote altruistic behaviour to some degree, and view selflessness as a virtue. Yet various studies suggest that religious orientation does not correlate well with the demonstration of concern and compassion for those needing help; indeed, it may discourage it in some situations (Batson and Gray, 1981).

In one study, the effects of different religious orientations were examined insofar as they influenced the willingness of individuals to provide help to a lonely woman, either in a situation where she expressed a desire for such help or in a situation where she expressly indicated that she did not want help (Batson and Gray, 1981). The data indicated that intrinsically-oriented religious people for whom religion was seen as an end in itself (i.e., who viewed their whole duty as serving God) offered help whether or not the person in need desired it, while those for whom religion was viewed as an open-ended quest to find ultimate values offered help only when it was wanted. Intrinsically-oriented religious people, then, may see providing help to others as a way of helping themselves achieve grace, or a place in Heaven. A subsequent study produced similar findings (Batson, Oleson, Weeks, Healy, Reeves, Jennings and Brown, 1989).

Rural-urban differences

Is a person from the country generally more inclined than a person from the city to help others? In a field study directed at rural-urban differences in helping, requests for help (e.g., "I wonder if you could tell me what time it is?") were made in downtown Toronto, in a Toronto suburb, and in a small town just outside Toronto (Rushton, 1978); the response rates, along with comparable data collected in New York City (Latané and Darley, 1970) are shown in the table on the next page. For every type of request, the percentage of people giving help dropped, moving from the small town to the suburbs to downtown. There was little difference between the results in downtown Toronto and New York City. Further evidence of significant rural/urban differences in helping comes from a review of 67 pertinent empirical studies. Steblay (1987) found that people in rural areas do indeed show significantly more willingness to help others in distress than do city dwellers.

However, even if people's behaviour in the city is less prosocial than that in the country, are the people themselves different, or is it the situation? Milgram (1970) argued that it is the latter, that people in the city, surrounded as they are by so many other people, out of necessity limit their social relationships to a minority of the populace. He argues that the urban person cannot afford to help every person who is in need and must be selective to survive in the urban culture. In addition, while rural people are considerably affected by rare emergency situations such as fires, the city-dweller becomes blasé about them, assuming that there are authorities who will deal with the situation. Furthermore, the city dweller who witnesses an emergency is more likely to be in or to think him/herself to be in the company of other witnesses (Latané and Darley, 1969). Moreover, the city person must compete for service (taxis, etc.) and norms develop (privacy, aloofness, etc.) to protect people from the constant interaction with others. It has been suggested that the intensity of urban stimuli (noise, pollution) may also lead to less prosocial behaviour. People living in cities have been found to be less trusting than people living in towns (Merrens, 1973; Milgram, 1970). Fischer (1976) suggests another reason why the city environment may discourage prosocial behaviour: A large city usually provides a great diversity of people—hence individuals may feel insecure among so many "dissimilar others," making social interaction less likely. Thus, in the city, there is a greater chance that the stranger who is in need of assistance will appear to be a member of an unfamiliar group, producing fear in the onlooker and resulting in less willingness to "get involved."

Rural-urban differences in helping behaviour

	Population Density							
	Low		Medium		High		High	
	Small Town		Toronto Suburbs		Toronto Inner City		New York City*	
Type of request	% Helping	N	% Helping	N	% Helping	N	% Helping	N
Time	97	92	95	150	91	272	85	92
Directions	97	85	90	150	88	276	85	90
Change	84	100	73	150	70	279	73	90
Name	51	65	39	150	26	246	29	277

*Based on data from Latané and Darley, 1970

SOURCE: Rushton, 1978

An Australian study (Amato, 1983) found that population size was a strong and consistent predictor of helping rate, with the most help occurring when the population of an area was small. However, the results of that study also suggested that urban lack of helpfulness was primarily limited to situations in which an individual was suddenly faced with the need to provide help to a stranger. This situation may be perceived as being more potentially dangerous by the city dweller than by the rural inhabitant. This research points to the importance of the *type* of helping and the *type* of situation in any examination of rural/urban differences in prosocial behaviour.

A Textbook of Social Psychology, Third Edition, J. E. Alcock, D. W. Carment, S. W. Sadava, © 1994. Used by permission of Prentice Hall Canada Inc.

TASK 5

Consolidating Information About the Topic

● WRITING NOTES BASED ON READ INFORMATION

FACTORS AFFECTING ALTRUISM (Part One)

In Task 4, you read about at least one of the factors that influence altruism, and learned about the other factors by listening to the members of your group and filling in a table with information.

Take a few moments now to make some notes on a separate sheet of paper about these factors.

Use your own words and do this from memory—do not refer back to the text or your notes.

TASK 6

More Specific Information

● USING SURVEY AND QUESTION STRATEGIES TO GET THE MAIN IDEA
● SUMMARIZING
● APPLYING READ INFORMATION TO CASES

BYSTANDER INTERVENTION

In a team of four, follow the steps below to get information from this academic reading.

1. Consider the four headings from this reading, which are printed below. Turn each heading into a question.

   a) The Presence of Others: The Lady in Distress

   _____

   _____

b) Ambiguity of the Situation: The Smoke-Filled Room

_____

_____

c) Diffusion of Responsibility: The Epileptic Seizure

_____

_____

d) Rewards and Costs of Helping

_____

_____

2. Read the text up to the first heading (The Presence of Others: The Lady in Distress). Then divide the next four sections among you. Using a separate sheet of paper, focus on the paragraph structure of your section carefully and follow these steps:

   a) Read the first sentence of each paragraph. Turn it into a question.

   b) Read each paragraph. Does it answer the question?

   c) Decide how much of the information presented you need in order to answer the question.

   d) Take **general** notes to answer the question.

3. Meet with classmates who have considered the same section of the reading. Compare your questions and notes for each paragraph. Clear up any differences.

4. Join your original team, and follow these steps to get full information:

   a) Sit with **one** group member. List your questions on a separate piece of paper, leaving plenty of space for notes between questions.

   b) Give your list of questions to your partner.

   c) Take turns asking each other the questions and answering them. Take **general** notes on the answers you hear.

   d) Meet with each group member in turn, following the same procedure.

   e) Pass your completed notes around the group and help each other to fill in any holes. Refer back to the text as needed.

5. Reread the real-life horror stories described in Task 3. Discuss how the information you have just learned can explain what happened in those stories. Share your discussion results with the class.

27,34

Of all the forms of prosocial behaviour, certainly the most dramatic—by virtue of either its presence or its absence—is intervention behaviour, that is, the behaviour of an individual who voluntarily goes to the aid of someone needing emergency assistance despite the possible risk of personal danger. Emergency situations share several common elements that make them somewhat unique (Darley and Latané, 1970):

(1) They typically involve threat or harm to a victim. The person who intervenes can at best prevent further damage or possibly return the situation to the way it was before the emergency occurred.

(2) Since recipients of such aid are rarely better off following an emergency than before it, the rewards for positive action are often non-existent. Yet the possible costs, including possible legal action or even death or injury, are high.

(3) They are rare events, so that few people have experience in dealing with them.

(4) They are unpredictable, occurring suddenly and without warning, and immediate action is required. Thus people usually cannot plan for emergencies or consult with others about how to respond. The urgency of the situation is in itself stressful.

(5) They vary widely in their form and in terms of what response is appropriate, making it impossible to prepare everyone by teaching people a short list of rules for how to deal with emergencies.

Unfortunately, there are all too many real-life examples of emergency situations in which someone has been in physical danger and other people have stood by and observed the individual being victimized while doing nothing to provide help. This is the "bystander effect": people witness an emergency but stand by passively and do nothing, their willingness to act, as we shall see later, inhibited by the presence of others. An important example is the Kitty Genovese murder. It is important because it was the first well-researched example of bystander inaction in an emergency situation. When asked later why they had not called the police, most of the witnesses to that murder said that they had indeed been afraid to get involved, but they seemed unable to furnish a basis for this fear. Various social scientists proposed a variety of *ad hoc* explanations for their inaction (Latané and Darley, 1970): alienation and apathy resulting from "depersonalization"; confusion of fantasy and reality brought about by a steady diet of television violence; even the vicarious gratification of sadistic impulses.

However, the witnesses were *not* apathetic. They did not turn away and ignore what was going on in the street below. Rather—

> Caught, fascinated, distressed, unwilling to act but unable to turn away, their behaviour was neither helpful nor heroic; but it was not indifferent or apathetic.... (Darley and Latané, 1970, p. 4).

Almost 15 years after the Genovese murder, a number of these witnesses were contacted. Again, they reported that they still felt responsible for Genovese's death (Walster, Walster and Berscheid, 1978).

The behaviour of these witnesses was very similar to that of any crowd that gathers around an accident victim, each waiting for someone else to take charge, to indicate what behaviour is appropriate. Sometimes people act; sometimes they do not. Yet, in any case, they are likely to experience distress. Several studies have found that when people witness another person being harmed, they show marked signs of emotional upheaval, such as gasping, running aimlessly around, sweating or trembling hands, chain-smoking, and an increase in galvanic skin response (Walster, Walster and Berscheid, 1978).

What accounts for bystander effect? If people are not apathetic, if their behaviour is not callous, what is it that holds them back from helping a person in distress? There are several possible answers to these questions.

The presence of others: The lady in distress

It might seem reasonable to assume that if an individual is the sort of person who is likely to come to someone's assistance in an emergency, that person would be even more likely to do so if there were other people about, for these other people might be expected to lend at least moral support. Yet, before accepting that conclusion, it would be wise to recall the literature on social facilitation: the presence of others facilitates simple or well-learned tasks, but interferes with complex or novel tasks. Emergency situations probably involve the latter and so there may be some reason to suspect that the presence of others may not always have a positive effect on the readiness of an individual to render assistance.

In one of the earliest experimental studies on the bystander effect (Latané and Rodin, 1969), the influence of the presence of others was clearly evident. In that experiment, subjects who thought they were participating in a market research study heard a woman who had just left them to go into an adjoining room "climb up" on a chair to get something, and then "fall down" and cry for help. (In fact, both the climb and fall were produced by a high fidelity tape recording.) The experimenters wanted to see whether or not and how soon subjects would come to her assistance. Subjects could go directly into her office (the two rooms were separated only by a curtain), could go out into the hallway to seek help, or could call to her to find out what they could do to help.

In one condition, each subject was alone. In a second condition, each subject was with a confederate who had been instructed to be as passive as possible, responding to any queries from the real subject in as natural but neutral a way as possible. At the sound of the crash, the confederate looked up, stared for a moment at the curtain, then shrugged his shoulders and went back to work. In a third condition, two real subjects who were strangers to each other were tested together, while a fourth condition involved two subjects who were friends.

The results showed that when assistance was offered, it was always direct, either going into the room (75 percent of the intervening subjects) or calling out to the woman to see if she wanted help (24 percent). The most notable finding was that while 70 percent of the subjects in the "alone" condition offered help, the presence of another person strongly reduced the frequency of intervention (the bystander effect): only seven percent of subjects paired with a passive confederate intervened, while only 40 percent of those in the "two strangers" condition offered help. The bystander effect was reduced when friends were paired together: in 70 percent of the pairs of friends there was at least one person who offered help. (However, it can be shown mathematically that if 70 percent of individuals who are alone are likely to intervene, then pairs of such individuals should contain at least one intervener 91 percent of the time. So, even with friends, the presence of another person is inhibitory.)

It seems strange at first that the presence of others inhibits rather than promotes helping. However, in post-experimental interviews, 59 percent of non-intervening subjects indicated that they were unsure about what had happened, while another 36 percent said they had thought that nothing serious had occurred. Perhaps people hesitate to help because the emergency situation seems ambiguous to them. Situational ambiguity merits a closer look; that subject is next.

Ambiguity of the situation: The smoke-filled room

Many emergency situations *are* ambiguous, and it is often surprisingly difficult to decide whether or not an emergency is occurring. If new neighbours in your apartment building seem to be having a squabble and you hear screams through the walls, do you intervene directly or call the police? It is difficult to decide whether or not someone is in trouble in such a situation, and usually a person does not want to look foolish by intervening if there is no emergency. Men are usually even more concerned than women are about the possibility of "doing the wrong thing" and looking foolish (Siem and Spence, 1986).

Although hearing a woman fall off a chair may not seem to present a particularly ambiguous situation, it must be remembered that the "accident" occurred out of sight of the subjects, and the sounds of climbing and falling and the calls for help were played over a tape recorder. It is possible that the reproduction did not sound totally real, thus producing some ambiguity. In fact, when the "Lady in Distress" study was repeated using live rather than taped noise, there was a high frequency of intervention (Staub, 1974). However, before concluding that the bystander effect simply reflects hesitation in the face of ambiguity, it must be remembered that the situation should have been equally ambiguous in all conditions. Nonetheless, the single subjects were much more willing to help, despite the ambiguity.

This outcome might suggest that the presence of others *contributes* to the ambiguity of the situation, that non-responding others lead an individual to wonder whether or not his or her own feeling that intervention is required is in error. Of course, if all those present feel the same way, then all may hold back.

The experiment described next explored whether or not the presence of others could produce inhibition, even when there was little ambiguity about the physical situation itself and even when a person might be at risk by doing nothing. Imagine yourself writing an examination. The examiner leaves the room; a few minutes later the room begins to fill up with smoke. What would you do? Would you leave the room (particularly if other examinees are doing nothing)? We would not expect such a situation, which carries some potential for personal harm, to give rise to a bystander effect. Latané and Darley (1968) created such a situation: Subjects who were engaged in filling out a questionnaire worked either alone, with two "passive" confederates, or with two other naive subjects. Several minutes after the person in charge left the room, smoke was introduced into the room via a small wall vent. By the end of four minutes, the room was filled with acrid smoke to the extent that it obscured vision.

While you might imagine that no one would wait around that long, that was not the case. Only 75 percent of the subjects in the alone condition left the room to report the smoke to someone. The others toughed it out, working on their questionnaires despite the cloud of smoke! While that in itself is very surprising, when a subject was in the company of two passive confederates, only one of ten subjects reported the smoke. The others coughed, rubbed their eyes, and even opened the window, but did not leave the room. When three naive subjects worked together, in only 38 percent of the groups did someone intervene. In fact naive subjects working together did not intervene significantly more often than a single naive subject working with two passive confederates.

These results support the interpretation that the passivity of others contributes to the ambiguity of the situation. In other words, we use the reactions of others to help decide whether or not there is an emergency and what action is appropriate. However, it might also be that the hesitancy to act was due to a fear of looking foolish by possibly doing the wrong thing.

To differentiate between inhibition brought about on one hand by the ambiguity produced by the inaction of others, and on the other by the fear of looking foolish, Ross and Braband (1973) carried out a study that used either a blind or a sighted confederate in each of two emergency conditions. In the "internal" emergency condition, the subject and the blind confederate worked in a room, which filled with odourless smoke; since the blind man could not see the smoke, he could not serve as a source of information about what reaction would be appropriate. In the "external" condition, the emergency was signalled by a scream from outside the room; in this case, the blind man would be aware of the emergency, and his reaction could serve as a guide to appropriate behaviour.

In fact, the subjects in the internal condition responded to the emergency just as quickly as did subjects in a control condition who worked alone. It could be argued, however, that these subjects were not concerned about acting inappropriately since the blind man could not see them. Yet this explanation is not tenable, for in the external condition, in which the blind man's reaction could be used as a guide, the subjects were inhibited to the same extent as when they were with a sighted confederate.

This experiment lends strong support to the notion that non-responding others inhibit a person's response because their inaction helps to define the situation as a non-emergency and thus makes intervention seem inappropriate. If non-intervention is largely caused by misinterpreting other people's reactions and believing that *they* know there is no cause for alarm, it follows that *not* knowing people's reactions should result in *not* being misled. Therefore, will people who know that others are aware of the possible emergency, but who cannot observe their reactions, be just as likely to intervene as people in an "alone" condition? This was the question addressed by the next experiment.

Diffusion of responsibility: The epileptic seizure

Each subject in this study (Darley and Latané, 1968) sat in a separate room and was told that he or she would take part in a discussion of personal problems associated with college life. The discussion was to be conducted by means of an intercom system,

ostensibly in order to protect the subjects' identities and spare them any embarrassment. Subjects had been told that the experimenter would not be listening to the initial discussion, and that a mechanical switching device would automatically give each subject in turn about two minutes to talk while all other microphones were switched off.

There was actually only one real subject at any one time. The other subjects, all confederates, had prerecorded their comments. From the point of view of the real subject, who believed that all the other speakers were actually present in the discussion, this is what occurred: The first person to speak discussed his adjustment difficulties and the fact that he was prone to epileptic seizures, especially when under stress. The next time it was his turn to speak, he became increasingly loud and incoherent and in a stuttering voice asked for help. Amid choking sounds, he stammered that he was going to die, called once more for help, and then was silent. When the seizure occurred, the real subject believed that all subjects could *hear* the seizure but that only the microphone of the seizure victim was switched on.

The major independent variable in this study was the apparent size of the group of participants, while the dependent variable was the time it took the subject to go and report the emergency to the experimenter. Comments made during the staged seizure and in later self-reports indicated that virtually all subjects believed the emergency was real. Yet the belief that other people were listening had a strong effect on both the rate and the speed of subjects' intervention (see the table below). Considerably more of the subjects in two-person (subject plus victim) groups reported the emergency than did people from the three-person groups, and people from the three-person groups responded more often than people from the six-person groups.

Thus it appears that a person is less likely to offer help if others are present or presumed to be present *even in the absence of ambiguity produced by*

Effects of group size on likelihood and speed of response				
Group size	N	% responding by end of seizure	Total % responding within six minutes	Average time in seconds
2 (subject and victim)	13	85	100	52
3 (subject, victim and one other)	26	62	85	93
6 (subject, victim and 4 others)	13	31	62	166
SOURCE: Latané and Darley, 1970				

the passivity of others. Subjects in this study who did not report the emergency did not show signs of apathy or indifference. In fact, when the experimenter finally entered the room to end the study, they appeared to be considerably emotionally upset and concerned for the victim. They found themselves in a conflict situation, worried about the victim and about the guilt they would feel if he was not helped, yet concerned about looking foolish, over-reacting, or ruining the experiment by leaving the room. When only the subject and the victim were involved, the victim's need could be met only by the subject, while when others seemed to be present (even in this case, via intercom), the subject had less responsibility in the matter. In other words, a *diffusion of responsibility* occurred: "Other people are listening, and so it is not up to me to take action: someone has probably already done something about it."

Three factors have emerged from the discussion so far. The bystander effect is the result of: (1) misperception of the emergency situation, based on the observation that others are not responding; (2) fear of doing the wrong thing and looking foolish; and (3) diffusion of responsibility. Many other studies and demonstrations have found results similar to those obtained by Latané and Darley. The bystander effect has been demonstrated on the streets of downtown Toronto, for instance (Ross, 1978): In one demonstration, which was filmed by a hidden camera, a confederate collapsed on busy Yonge Street. Many people walked by, stepping around the man, before someone finally stopped to offer help. In another demonstration, a confederate grabbed another confederate's purse in front of City Hall, in full view of a lunchtime crowd. The victim called for people to stop him, as she ran after him. No help was forthcoming. It had been expected that for each demonstration, several trials would have to be made before such blatant non-intervention could be observed and filmed. In fact, in each case, only one trial was necessary. (The reader is invited to think about the ethical considerations inherent in carrying out such demonstrations.)

The social inhibition of helping is a remarkably consistent phenomenon and, in general, a victim stands a greater chance of being helped when only a single person witnesses the emergency (Latané and Nida, 1981).

Rewards and costs of helping

A classic experiment carried out in New York has revealed yet another aspect of the bystander effect. This field experiment, taking place in a city with no outstanding reputation for altruism, found that no bystander effect occurred when a confederate of the experimenter collapsed on a moving subway car. The experiment examined the effects of certain characteristics of a victim (whether he appeared drunk or ill, whether he was Black or White) on the amount of help given. It was expected that the "drunk" confederate (who carried a bottle in a paper bag and who smelled of alcohol) would elicit less aid than an ill one (carrying a cane) since it was assumed people might anticipate the drunk becoming disgusting, embarrassing, or violent. The most surprising outcome was that there was a generally high rate of help-giving in all conditions. In fact, the "ill" person received help on 95 percent of the trials, and even the "drunk" was helped on half the trials. Moreover, when help was given, on 60 percent of those occasions more than one person helped. Since the ill person was not thought to be ill by choice while the drunk was clearly in need of help as a result of his own actions, people may have been less willing to help the drunk because he "deserved" his suffering (Piliavin, Rodin and Piliavin, 1969).

Why was so much inaction observed in the Darley and Latané laboratory research but not in the Piliavin field experiment? Why was there less diffusion of responsibility on the subway? There were important differences between the two sets of studies. First, the victim was in full view in the Piliavin study; thus the need for help was less ambiguous. Second, the natural groups were considerably larger than the laboratory groups. Thus any diffusion of responsibility that might have occurred may have been *more* than offset by the increased probability of *someone* actually helping in a large group. In other words, the larger number of bystanders in the subway study may have increased the probability of getting a prosocial response from someone (Piliavin *et al.*, 1972). Moreover, it was much more difficult for the subjects in the Piliavin study to leave the area than it was for participants in the Latané and Darley studies to avoid the victim. This difference bears more examination.

Whether or not a person helps another may depend on how easily he or she can avoid the helping situation. In an experiment designed to examine this hypothesis (Staub, 1974), a confederate collapsed, holding either his chest or his knees (to vary the apparent seriousness of his condition) either in the pathway of a pedestrian (difficult escape), or across the street (easy escape). As can be seen in the table on the next page, many more people helped when escape from the situation was difficult than when it was easy. In fact, the person with the apparent "heart attack" was almost always approached in the difficult escape condition. The results suggest that the perceived degree of need for help also influenced helping. More people approached the apparent coronary victim. Interestingly enough, a fat confederate who clutched his chest was more likely to receive aid than a non-obese confederate. It turned out that subjects more often considered the problem to be a coronary one when the victim was obese. Recall that in the Piliavin study, people could not easily escape; it was several minutes to the next stop.

All that being said, it is sobering to learn that 30 or more passengers, including some hefty men, watched passively as three youths beat up a man in a moving subway car in Toronto in September 1973; no one even stood up or spoke. They watched in silence. While the New York subway riders had relatively little to lose by helping a sick person or a drunk, there is more to risk if we intervene in a fight. Thus, besides the factors already discussed—

Number of people helping or refusing to help in the 1974 Staub study				
	Bad knee		Bad heart	
	Help	No help	Help	No help
Easy escape	2	12	5	7
Difficult escape	9	7	14	2
SOURCE: Staub, 1974				

ambiguity, fear of looking foolish, diffusion of responsibility, difficulty of avoidance—it is clear that the readiness to help will be strongly affected by the potential costs to the helper.

A *Textbook of Social Psychology*, Third Edition, J. E. Alcock, D. W. Carment, S. W. Sadava, © 1994. Used by permission of Prentice Hall Canada Inc.

TASK 7

Listening to Clarify

- GUIDED NOTETAKING
- LISTENING TO CONFIRM AND CLARIFY READ INFORMATION

THE BYSTANDER EFFECT: A REVIEW

1. Listen to the lecture to confirm and clarify information about the bystander effect. Take notes using the headings below.

THE PRESENCE OF OTHERS

AMBIGUITY OF THE SITUATION

DIFFUSION OF RESPONSIBILITY

FIGHTING THE EFFECT

2. Check and compare your notes with those of a partner.

3. Return to Task 6 and add or change the information that you recorded there, based on your lecture notes.

4. As a class, discuss the suggestions for fighting the effect. Can you add to those suggestions? Add them to your list above.

TASK 8

Consolidating Information

● WRITING NOTES BASED ON READ INFORMATION

FACTORS AFFECTING ALTRUISM (Part Two)

In Tasks 6 and 7, you read and listened to more information about the factors affecting altruism.

Take a few moments to make notes here.

Use your own words and do this from memory—do not refer back to the text or your notes.

TASK 9

Applying the Information

- COLLABORATING ON NARRATIVE WRITING
- APPLYING READ INFORMATION TO CASES

1. Look at these four sentences, the beginning of four short stories:
   - The school bus hit the water with a splash.
   - We could hear a child crying through the roar of the fire.
   - The old woman obviously couldn't get away from the oncoming traffic.
   - They told us that Jane had walked into the forest two days earlier.

2. Decide which one of these stories you would like to write, and then form a group of three or four people who want to write the same one. Sit in a circle. **Your story should include ideas covered in this unit.**

3. Copy the first sentence of the story onto a piece of paper.

4. Write a second sentence for the story.

5. Pass your piece of paper to the person on your right, and take the piece of paper from the person on your left.

6. Read the two sentences on the paper, and add a third sentence.

7. Pass the piece of paper to the person on your right, take the piece of paper from the person on your left, read the three sentences, and add a fourth one.

8. Continue writing sentences and passing the pieces of paper until you receive a paper with **12** sentences on it.

9. Write an ending for the story in front of you.

10. As a group, look at all the stories you have produced and decide which one is the best.

11. Rewrite the story to make it as clear and interesting as possible.

12. Divide the story into parts and practise telling it as a group.

13. Tell the story to another group, and answer any questions that the group members may have about it.

Essay

Your final assignment for this unit is to write an essay responding to the following statement:

Altruism is a result of many factors, and does not just depend on individual personality.

The following steps will help you to prepare.

1. To begin, take a look at the lists of factors influencing altruism. As well, review the research evidence relating to the five main influences as well as bystander intervention. You may also wish to include some of the real-life horror stories from Task 3 as examples.

2. With a partner, go through your notes and answers from the unit. Decide which information is **most useful** for your essay. You will probably want to select only the most important factors because the essay will be too long if you include all the information.

3. List your points on a separate piece of paper. Discuss them with a partner. Focus on how to **organize** the information effectively.

   Here are some suggestions to help you write a convincing academic argument:

   - Decide whether you **agree or disagree** with the statement.
   - In the **introduction**, start with a **thesis statement**, and then list the factors you will discuss to prove your thesis.
   - Make each paragraph of the body of the essay a discussion of **one** factor. Start these paragraphs with a topic sentence introducing the factor. Then, describe how the factor affects altruism. Be sure to explain the factor and its connection to altruism clearly.
   - Write a brief **conclusion** restating your thesis and pointing out how you proved it. List the factors again in the conclusion.
   - It can help to share each paragraph with a partner or two. Ask each other questions about the points you have made. These questions can help you to expand the information and explain in more depth.
   - Alternatively, turn your paper over after each paragraph and write three to five questions about the information. By answering these questions, you will be expanding the information and deepening your explanation.

4. At each step of the writing process, discuss your writing with a classmate or two. If your partners do not understand what you have written, you may need to revise the writing in some parts.

5. **Edit** the essay for grammar and vocabulary problems only after you have finished organizing it and clarifying the points you have made. Check particular language problems with the teacher.

6. **Evaluate** your work when you feel you have finished. Use the following questions to help you decide how well you did.

a) What are the strengths of the essay?

b) What are the weak parts, or what would you change if you could?

c) What type of feedback do you want from the teacher?

d) Do you feel that the essay is really responding to the statement?

e) Do you have a clearly stated thesis?

f) Have you listed the factors at the beginning?

g) Does each paragraph have a topic sentence?

h) Does each paragraph fully explain the factor being discussed?

i) Is the conclusion a good restatement of the thesis, and does it list the factors again?

9 Tides: Can We Use Them?

UNIT OVERVIEW

This unit focuses on the earth's ocean tides, and ways to use them for power generation. It involves reading about the relationships among the earth, moon, and sun, and includes some descriptions of how tides could be harnessed to provide electricity. The unit leads to a lot of discussion as you work closely together to collect information from the readings and complete the final task.

The final project in this unit is to create a set of posters and a presentation illustrating the causes of tides and how tidal power could be harnessed.

You should turn to the project description at the end of the unit regularly to see how much information and how many skills you need to help you complete it.

READING *You will read for information, and skim and scan academic text to get the most important information for your purposes. You will discuss information gained by skimming, and analyse information paragraph by paragraph.*

LISTENING *You will listen to a discussion of a specific example illustrating some aspects of the topic.*

WRITING *You will write short answers to tasks presented in the unit. You will write captions and brief explanations for the final project to help present the unit material.*

SPEAKING *You will discuss information presented in the unit. You will talk and work together to create the final presentation, sharing the task of preparing a visual explanation of the topic and a brief group presentation.*

TO BEGIN, TURN THE PAGE AND START THINKING ABOUT AND DISCUSSING THE TOPIC IN GENERAL.

Introduction to the Topic

● SHARING KNOWLEDGE
AND EXPERIENCE

DISCUSSING TIDES

1. In a group of three, discuss the following questions. Then share the results of your discussion with the class. Use the spaces below to record any notes from your discussions.

a) What influences does the moon have on the earth?

b) Have you ever witnessed the rising and falling of the tides at the seacoast? If so, where?

c) How frequently do tides rise and fall? Is there a regular natural schedule for tides in the earth's seas and oceans?

d) What effects do tides have on our lives?

e) Do tides have any potential value of tides for our future?

2. Now see how many of the words below you can under-stand in your group without referring to a dictionary. Write a synonym or a brief definition for each.

gravity _____

tide _____

lunar _____

bulge _____

elongated _____

axis _____

basin _____

orbit _____

Getting Introductory Information by Reading, Illustrating

- SCANNING TO GET THE MAIN IDEA
- TRANSFERRING TEXTUAL INFORMATION TO GRAPHIC FORM

TIDES

You will cover the information in this reading, taken from a physics textbook, paragraph by paragraph. There are six paragraphs.

1. Follow these steps for each paragraph:

   a) Take **two minutes** to scan it, using the paragraph descriptions below to help you search for information.

   b) Jot down a few notes **without looking back at the paragraph.**

   c) Discuss the information with a partner.

   d) Refer back to the paragraph to help you confirm what you understood.

   - Paragraph 1 discusses what tides are.

   - Paragraph 2 explains the causes of tides.

   - Paragraph 3 explains the relationship between gravity and tides. Look for a definition of **tidal bulge**.

   - Paragraph 4 explains why the waters of the earth rise and fall with the movements of the earth and moon.

   - Paragraph 5 explains the relationship among the sun, the moon, and the tides. Look for definitions of **spring tides** and **neap tides**.

- Paragraph 6 discusses **tidal force**. Look for an example of the effect of tidal force.

2. Now that you have dealt with all six paragraphs, go back and read the text as a whole. Clear up any gaps in your notes with reference to the text.

3. To consolidate the information you have learned, work with a partner. On a separate sheet of paper, draw a simple diagram to illustrate the main points of what you have read. Show the earth, the moon, directions of gravitational pulls, and the movement of the earth's oceans.

READING | TIDES

Most people are familiar with the daily fluctuation in ocean level known as the tides. At most coastal locations on Earth, there are two low tides and two high tides each day. The "height" of the tides—the magnitude of the variation in sea level—can range from a few centimeters to many meters, depending on the location on Earth and time of year. The height of a typical tide on the open ocean is about a meter. An enormous amount of energy is contained in the daily motion of the oceans, constantly eroding and reshaping our planet's coastlines.

What causes the tides? A clue comes from the fact that they exhibit daily, monthly, and yearly cycles. In fact, the tides are a direct result of the gravitational influence of the Moon and the Sun on the Earth. We have already seen how gravity keeps the Earth and Moon in orbit about one another, and both in orbit around the Sun. For simplicity, let us first consider just the interaction between Earth and the Moon.

Recall that the strength of gravity depends on the distance separating any two objects. Thus, different parts of the Earth feel slightly different pulls due to the Moon's gravity, depending on their distance from the Moon. For example, the Moon's gravitational attraction is greater on the side of Earth that faces the Moon than on the opposite side, some 13,000 km farther away. This difference in the gravitational force is small—only about 3 percent—but it produces a noticeable effect—a tidal bulge. The Earth becomes slightly elongated, with the long axis of the distortion pointing toward the Moon, as illustrated in Figure 1.

The liquid portions of the Earth undergo greater deformation than the solid portions because liquid can more easily move around on the surface. Thus, the ocean becomes a little deeper in some places (along the line joining the Earth to the Moon) and shallower in others (perpendicular to this line). The daily tides we see result as the Earth rotates beneath this deformation. Notice in Figure 1 that the side of Earth *opposite* the Moon also experiences a tidal bulge. The different gravitational pulls—greatest on that part of Earth closest to the Moon, weaker at the Earth's center, and weakest of all on the Earth's opposite side—cause average tides on either side of our planet to be approximately equal in height. On the side nearer the Moon, the ocean water is pulled slightly toward the Moon. On the opposite side, the ocean water is literally left behind as the Earth is pulled closer to the Moon. Thus, high tide occurs *twice*, not once, every day.

Both the Moon and the Sun exert tidal forces on our planet. Even though the Sun is roughly 375 times farther away from Earth than is the Moon, its mass is so much greater (by about a factor of 27 million) that its tidal influence is still significant—about half that of the Moon. Thus, instead of one tidal bulge, there are actually two—one pointing toward the Moon, the other toward the Sun—and the interaction between them accounts for the changes in the height of the tides over the course of a month or a year. When the Earth, Moon, and Sun are roughly lined up—at new or full Moon—the gravitational effects reinforce one another and the highest tides occur. These tides are known as *spring tides*. When the Earth–Moon line is perpendicular to the Earth–Sun line (at the first and third quarters), the daily tides are smallest. These are termed *neap tides*. The relative orientations of the Earth, Sun, and Moon at times of spring and neap tides are illustrated in Figure 2.

The variation of the Moon's gravity across the Earth is an example of a *differential*, or **tidal**, **force**. The *average* gravitational interaction between two bodies determines their orbit around one another. However, the *tidal force*, superimposed on that average, tends to deform the bodies themselves. It diminishes very rapidly with increasing distance. We will see many examples in this book of situations where tidal forces are critically important in understanding astronomical phenomena. Notice that we still use the word *tidal* in these other contexts, even though we are not discussing oceanic tides, and possibly not even planets at all.

FIGURE 1

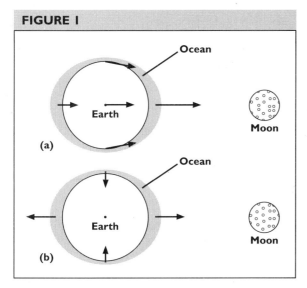

This exaggerated illustration shows how the Moon induces tides on both the near and the far sides of the Earth. The lengths of the straight arrows indicate the relative strengths of the Moon's gravitational pull on various parts of Earth. (a) The lunar gravitational forces acting on several different locations on and in the Earth. The force is greatest on the side nearest the Moon and smallest on the opposite side. (b) The difference between the lunar forces experienced at those same locations and the force acting on the Earth's center. The arrows represent the force with which the Moon tends to pull matter away from, or squeeze it toward, the center of our planet. Material on the side of Earth nearest the Moon tends to be pulled away from the center, while material on the far side is "left behind" as the Earth itself is tugged toward the Moon. A bulge forms as a result of this pushing and pulling. High and low tides result, twice per day, as the Earth rotates beneath the bulges in Earth's oceans.

FIGURE 2

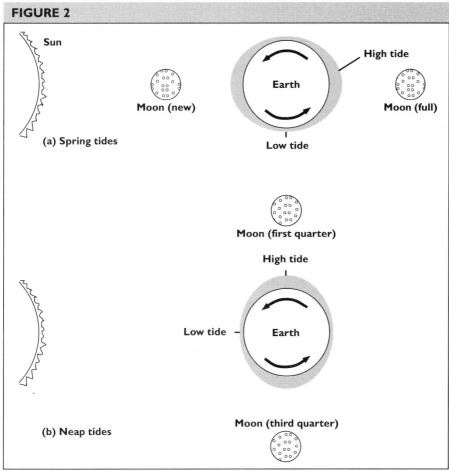

The combined effects of the Sun and the Moon produce variations in the high and low tides. (a) When the Moon is full (or new), the Earth, Moon, and Sun are approximately aligned, and the tidal bulges raised in Earth's oceans by the Moon and the Sun reinforce one another. (b) At first (or third) quarter Moon, the tidal effects of the Moon and the Sun partially cancel, and the tides are smallest. The Moon's tidal effect is greater than that of the Sun, so the net bulge points toward the Moon.

TASK 3

Building on What Is Read, Illustrating

- DETERMINING NEW AND OLD INFORMATION IN A TEXT
- READING FOR COMPLETE INFORMATION
- TRANFERRING TEXTUAL INFORMATION TO GRAPHIC FORM

1. Before reading the following excerpt from an astronomy textbook, take a few moments, in a small group, to discuss the information from the previous reading. Focus on these questions and write short answers for each.

   a) What are tides?

   _____

   _____

   b) How frequent are tides?

   _____

   c) What causes tides?

   _____

   _____

   d) How does the relationship between the moon and earth cause tides?

   _____

   _____

   e) What is the influence of the sun on tides?

   _____

   _____

2. Now, take **20 minutes** to read through this text. Place a mark in the margin beside each paragraph while you are reading to indicate either

   - information already provided in the first reading (use a check mark ✓)
   - new information (use an asterisk ✱)

3. Compare your margin marks with those of a partner, and clear up any differences. Share the results of this discussion with the class.

4. In a group of three, go back and study the text to answer the following questions, one for each paragraph. Discuss the questions and paragraphs together. Use the spaces provided to record your notes.

   PARAGRAPH 1. What is the time cycle for tides? Why is it like this?

PARAGRAPH 2. How does the pull of the moon on the earth affect the oceans?

PARAGRAPH 3. What is the effect of the pull of the moon on waters that are

• on the side of the earth nearest the moon?

• on the side of the earth farthest from the moon?

PARAGRAPH 4. What is the effect of the pull of the moon on water that is the same distance from the moon as the earth's centre?

PARAGRAPH 5. Why is it that oceans show the effects of the pull of the moon, but we do not?

PARAGRAPH 6. What are the possibilities for electrical power from tides? What about the spring tides in the Bay of Fundy?

5. In your group, refer back to the diagram you created at the end of Task 2. On a separate sheet of paper, create a new diagram to illustrate the phenomenon of tides more fully. Share it with the class.

Since the dawn of navigation, mariners have marked deep channels in ports and rivers to avoid sandbars and mud flats at low tide. For centuries port cities have kept records of the times and levels of high and low tides. The table below lists the high and low tides at the Battery in New York City for several days. It reveals a general pattern: There are usually two high tides and two low tides each day; the high tides are about 12 hours and 25 minutes apart, as are the low tides. This pattern was the key to discovering the cause of the tides. While 24 hours is the period of the earth's rotation with respect to the sun (sunrise to sunrise, say), 24 hours and 50 minutes is the earth's rotation period with respect to the moon (or moonrise to moonrise). This is twice the tidal period of 12 hours and 25 minutes, and it leads to the fact that *the moon is the principal cause of the ocean's tides.*

The earth and moon pull on each other, according to Newton's law of gravity, with exactly the same amount of force. So as the moon glides along on its large orbit, the earth, with about 81 times the mass of the moon, performs a miniature orbit of its own (Figure 1). Both are in free fall around each other! At the same time, each body is immersed in the other's gravitational field, and the strength of these fields varies somewhat over their surfaces and throughout their bodies. Let's assume for now that the earth is perfectly rigid and accelerates toward the moon at a rate determined by the *average* pull on it. The oceans, which are not rigid, cover about 70% of earth's surface and are all connected. Because they are connected, they act much like a bowl of jello does when a spoon touches it; if the surface of the water goes down somewhere, it has to rise somewhere else.

Figure 2 shows some details of the moon's attraction. On the side of earth nearest the moon, the moon's pull on the ocean waters is slightly stronger than its pull on the rigid earth below. On the side of earth farthest from the moon, the moon's pull on the ocean waters is weaker than its pull on earth. The result is that ocean water nearest the moon actually weighs less by a small percentage because of the moon's gravity. If earth's gravity weren't holding it to the surface, that part of the ocean would "outrun" the earth toward the moon. The water on the far side of the earth is lighter as well because if earth's gravity didn't hold it against the surface, earth would "outrun" those waters toward the moon, leaving them behind. You can feel this effect in an elevator that's accelerating downward; you feel lighter. You still stay on the elevator floor, of course, and the ocean still stays on the surface of the earth, but the "reduced weight" effect is real in both cases.

At the same time, ocean water that is about the same distance from the moon as earth's center is slightly heavier due to the moon's gravity. That's because the moon's pull in that area isn't horizontal; it has a downward component that presses the ocean water directly against the surface, adding to its weight (Figure 3).

Tides at the Battery, New York, 1982

October 26	high	3:11 a.m.
	low	9:36 a.m.
	high	3:22 p.m.
	low	10:12 p.m.
October 27	high	4:10 a.m.
	low	10:28 a.m.
	high	4:23 p.m.
	low	10:57 p.m.
October 28	high	5:02 a.m.
	low	11:16 a.m.

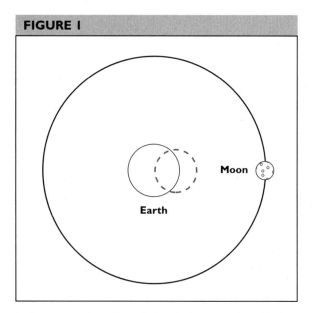

FIGURE 1

As the moon orbits earth, earth travels along a smaller orbit of the same shape. Action equals reaction with gravity as with any other force. Earth's larger mass means its acceleration, and hence its orbit, are much smaller than the moon's. $M_E A_E = M_M A_M$ (The moon's orbit in this drawing is not to scale.)

The effect of all those forces is to stretch the oceans out a tiny bit along the straight line between the centers of the earth and moon, and to squeeze them in between. As a result, the ocean's surface becomes, to a very small degree, football-shaped. To understand this we can look at the gravitational force at points on the surface relative to the *average* gravitational force from the moon on the earth. If the average force for the rigid earth is subtracted from all the force vectors in its surface, Figure 4 is the result. This force is called the moon's **tidal force** at the surface of earth. This tidal force is very small, or else you would feel heavier or lighter as the earth's rotation took you through the regions of Figure 4. But the oceans respond to these tiny forces over their immense areas, and tiny bulges and dips are the result—no drop of water moves very far, but the oceans' surfaces rise and fall as earth's rotation carries them through the areas of different tidal force. The bulges in the oceans cause high tides along the shores of continents and islands as earth rotates. The depressions, encountered about six hours after each high tide, cause the low tides (Figure 5).

Tides From the Sun

Ocean tides at mid-ocean due to the moon amount to only 1 1/2 feet from high to low. The sun, too, pulls harder on the ocean waters nearest it and less on those farthest away; its high-to-low tides amount to about 1 foot at mid-ocean. Its tides are smaller than the moon's even though the sun's net

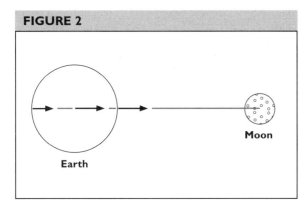

FIGURE 2

A comparison of the relative strengths of the moon's gravitational pull at three points, the closest and farthest points to the moon from earth's surface and at the center of the earth. (The moon is actually much farther away from the earth than shown here, and the forces are more nearly the same at the three points.)

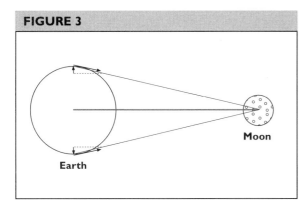

FIGURE 3

At points on earth's surface that are perpendicular to the earth–moon line, the moon's gravitational pull has a small component that presses matter toward earth's center, making things slightly heavier there. (Drawing not to scale.)

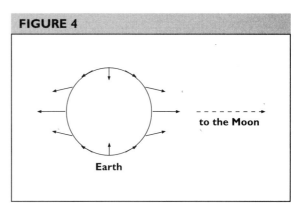

FIGURE 4

If the vector forces at earth's surface due to the moon's gravity are drawn and the pull of the moon's gravity at earth's center is subtracted from each, the result is the action of the moon's gravity with respect to the earth's center. That force is called the tidal force. It causes a bulge (high tide) in the oceans under the moon and on the opposite side from the moon, and low-tide regions in between.

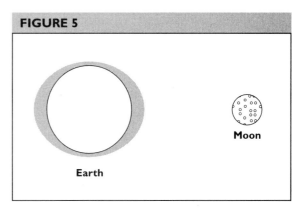

FIGURE 5

The (exaggerated) shape of earth's oceans because of the moon's tidal force as in Figure 4. (The distortions caused by earth's rotation are not shown.)

gravitational pull on earth is far stronger! This is because the *percentage difference* in the sun's force of gravity from one side of the earth to the other is less than the moon's, and that is what causes the tides. When the sun and moon tides align, at full moon and new moon, as in Figure 6 a and b, the tides swing 2 1/2 feet and are called *spring tides*. At first quarter moon or third quarter moon (Figure 6 c), their tides subtract; that is, the bulges due to the sun occur in the depressions due to the moon and vice versa, and the tides are only about 1/2 foot. These are called *neap tides*. Coastline indentations, such as bays and rivers, can funnel the rising tidal waters and bring about a large horizontal current and a higher rise in the local water level. A noteworthy example is the Bay of Fundy in Nova Scotia, where during spring tides the water sometimes rises 50 feet from low tide to high tide! These enormous volumes of water can be temporarily trapped and sent through turbines which drive electrical generators. In France one such plant has been in operation since 1966, generating the electrical needs of Brittany. Another smaller plant is operated in the former Soviet Union, and studies are underway for a tidal plant along the coast of Maine. Unfortunately, only 30 locations world-wide have tides large enough to generate significant power, so this alternative source of energy is very limited.

FIGURE 6

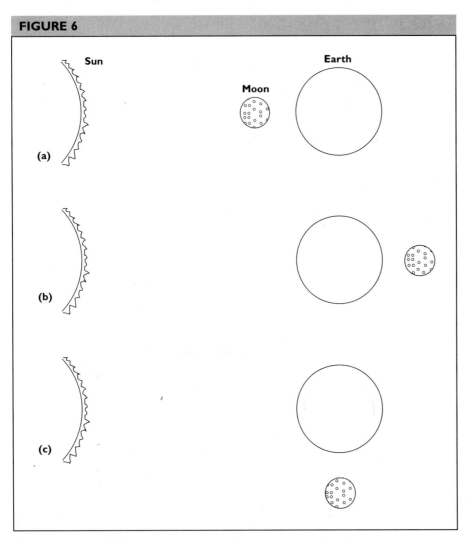

(a) New moon and (b) full moon cause tides that align with the sun's tides, giving the very large "spring" tides. (c) Neap tides, very low tides, occur when the earth–sun line makes a right angle with the earth–moon line. That happens when the moon is in its first or third quarter phase. (Drawing not to scale.)

Physics: A Window on Our World, Third Edition, by Boleman, Jay, © 1995. Reprinted by permission of Prentice-Hall, Inc., Upper Saddle River, N.J.

TASK 4

Listening to an Example

- LISTENING FOR TOPICAL VOCABULARY AND CONCEPTS IN A SPECIFIC CONTEXT
- LISTENING TO DESCRIPTION OF PROCESSES

THE BAY OF FUNDY AND THE PHENOMENON OF RESONANCE

1. Listen carefully to the description of the Fundy tidal system and define these terms:

tidal bore _____

_____

_____

spring tides _____

_____

_____

oscillation _____

_____

_____

resonance _____

_____

_____

diurnal _____

_____

_____

2. Listen again and make notes on the Fundy system using the outline below.

   THE FUNDY BORE

   significance

   location

THE MINAS BASIN

location

height of tides

volume of water

OSCILLATION AND RESONANCE IN FUNDY

oscillation

resonance

THE FUNNEL

effect on tides

3. Now that you have listened to and written an outline of the information, prepare a brief talk with a partner, summarizing the information in the lecture. Be sure to use and define the key terms and describe the Fundy system fully. Use the space below for your notes.

4. Present your talk to another pair. Give each other feedback on the accuracy of the information and the clarity of the explanation.

TASK 5

Getting Specific Information About the Topic, Illustrating

- READING FOR COMPLETE INFORMATION
- TRANSFERRING TEXTUAL INFORMATION TO GRAPHIC FORM

ENERGY IN THE TIDES

1. Read the following text, taken from a textbook on energy, and answer the questions below.

   a) What has to be built to get energy from tides?

   _____

   _____

   _____

   b) What factor determines the amount of energy possible from a hydroelectric plant using tides?

   _____

   _____

   _____

   c) Is tidal power a large proportion of the water energy in the world?

   _____

   _____

   _____

d) What is **two-way generation**?

_____

_____

_____

e) What is one advantage of two-way generation?

_____

_____

f) How does two-way generation use a reservoir?

_____

_____

g) Explain **resonance**. How does it relate to tides?

_____

_____

h) What are some potential dangers of tidal hydroelectrical development of the Minas Basin?

_____

_____

_____

i) What are the author's conclusions about the potential of tidal electrical power?

_____

_____

_____

2. Discuss your answers in a group of three, and clear up any differences with reference to the text. Discuss the answers as a class.

3. In your group, create a simple diagram on a separate sheet of paper to illustrate how two-way generation would work in a tidal basin. Share your illustration with the class.

Tidal energy arises from the interaction of the Sun (and the Moon, whose effect is twice as large) with Earth. The oscillatory flow of water in filling and emptying a partly enclosed region along a coast can be tapped to produce electricity. This energy may be made available by cutting off the basin with dams to create a water level difference. Of course, the total amount of energy available depends strongly on the difference between the high and low tide levels, the *tidal range,* because it uses the potential energy generated by the rise and fall of the tides to generate hydroelectricity.

Use of tidal energy is not new. Before 1100, tide mills operated on the European coast. The total world tidal energy available is estimated to be 2.9 $TkWh_e$ and is only about 1% of the world's available water power. The largest facility in operation, at 240-MW installed capacity, is at La Rance, France. It has a tidal range of ~8 m and produces about half a billion kWh_e yearly (about 20% of the maximum available energy and 90% of the design value). Overall, for the world's operating units there is a load factor of 22% to 35%.

The energy could be tapped by taking power only when the basin is emptying, or both as it fills and empties. Two-way generation is not advantageous compared to one-way because of the limitation of available head from obstructing inflow. However, two-way generation operates over a longer time, sending a steadier supply to the grid, and so may be preferable. A 5% to 15% energy gain is possible when water is pumped into the reservoir near high tide. It is then let out near low tide, with a large increase in energy.

In the Bay of Fundy, which has a 15-m average tidal range, a plant was proposed for the Minas Basin; if built, it would provide about 15 $GkWh_e$ yearly. The total potential electric generation capability of the entire Bay of Fundy system is between 30 and 60 GWh/year. The scheme would consist of 128 turbines with an installed capacity of 5 GW_e, and with the intermittent character of the tidal rise and fall, the power output would average ~1.75 GW_e. The Bay of Fundy has the largest tidal range in the world, which is due to the resonance between the tidal forcing and the Gulf of Maine, of which Fundy is a part. (*Resonance* refers to what happens to the response amplitude at some particular frequency of forcing—for example, if your tires are out of balance, the imbalance provides a periodic jar; the jarring can cause the car to shake as if it would fall apart at one particular speed. If you speed up or slow down, the shaking vanishes. You have just found a resonant frequency for your car. Bodies of

TAPPING TIDAL ENERGY

Energy from the tides is generated in much the same way as hydroelectric energy from dams is generated. Tidal basins (partly enclosed river mouths, bays, and so on) empty and fill with the tides. If the basins are closed off by dams, water level differences will exist between the basin and the ocean that could be used to run turbines.

The total amount of energy available from such an enclosed basin is *MGh*, where *M* is the mass of extra water held by the basin at high tide as compared to low tide, *g* is the acceleration of gravity (9.82 m/s²), and *h* (the tidal range) is the difference in heights between high and low tide. The mass *M* of water stored in the basin is proportional to the surface area of the basin and to *h*. Thus the mass of captured water is given by the density of seawater (1030 kg/m³) multiplied by the volume of water captured by the dam; the volume is (area) x *h*; thus

$$M = \text{(density of water)} \times \text{(area)} \times h.$$

This means that the stored energy grows as the square of *h*.

$$\text{stored energy} = Mgh$$
$$= \text{(density of water)} \times \text{(area)} \times h \times gh$$
$$= \text{(density of water)} \times \text{(area)} \times gh^2.$$

For this reason, regions with high tidal ranges, such as the Bay of Fundy, have the greatest potential for energy production. Clearly, the area is also important, which is why all possibilities considered are large bodies of water.

The energy actually available is generally only a fraction of the maximum potential. The operation at La Rance, one of only two working tidal power installations, produces between 20% and 25% of the theoretical maximum. Still, although tidal energy is only a minor *world* energy resource, locally it could have a large impact indeed. The closing of the San Jose Bay in Argentina; Mont Saint-Michel in France; Severn in England; Cook Inlet in Alaska; and the White Sea, the Sea of Okhotsk, and the Penzhinsk Gulf in Russia could produce average power in the gigawatt range. Other potential local sources are relatively minor compared to these. Most of these, however, would be too expensive to develop.

water can resonate, too. Ask any child who used a washcloth to push on water in the bathtub with just the right frequency to make a huge wave go over the edge of the bathtub onto the floor!)

The Gulf of Maine has a natural period of about 13.3 hours, while the Moon-caused tidal period is 12.4 hours. This near-match causes the huge water flow: about $1/40$ $(km)^3/s$. There is a possible problem with the Minas Basin project. Models indicate that closing off the Minas Basin would decrease the natural period of the Gulf of Maine, causing an increase in the tidal range as a result of the closer match. Therefore, tides would be higher as far south as Cape Cod. This project might even change tides in Britain, although by only a few millimeters. The effect on the Georges Bank, a major world fishery, is still to be determined. So far, only a test facility is operating.

The costs of tidal energy are not going to drop very much because of the extensive construction and operational experience. There also are fewer surprises with this form of energy, and it is the only alternative that can be clearly economic at present.

Energy by Aubrecht, © 1994. Reprinted by permission of Prentice-Hall, Inc., Upper Saddle River, NJ.

Poster Presentation

1. Form pairs to work together on a set of posters illustrating the relationships among the moon, sun, and earth, and how tides are caused. You should also include illustrations and information about hydroelectrical power generation from tidal basins, showing two-way generation.

2. Review the information covered in this unit.

3. Work together to try to decide how to balance illustrations and text in your posters to make an effective presentation.

Here are some tips to help you in your poster design:

- The theme of each poster should be instantly understood, without the viewer having to study the posters carefully.

- Use a simple combination of pictures, words, and other means to communicate your idea.

- You must draw your own diagrams, and write labels and captions for them in your own words.

- Be creative. Use clever illustrations and surprising or interesting words.

- Keep your eyes open outside of class to notice features of posters that seem useful and interesting.

4. After creating the posters, prepare a brief oral description of the information. Use the following questions to help you refine both the posters and the presentation. Use them as well to practise and rehearse.

CONTENT

- Do the posters and presentation clearly state the topics?
- Do the posters have useful and interesting illustrations? Are they understandable?
- Does the presentation have enough information? Is it understandable?

ORGANIZATION

- Discuss how the group and the individual members have organized the task and the information.
- Is there a logical sequence of points to build an explanation of tides and tidal power?
- Does the set of posters have a clear beginning, middle, and end? Is the information organized for the best effect?
- Does the presentation have a clear beginning, middle, and end? Is the information organized for the best effect?
- Is any information missing? Are any steps of explanation missing?

LANGUAGE AND DELIVERY

- Are there any pronunciation problems that make the presentation hard to understand?
- Are the group members presenting as a group?

10 Race and Ethnic Relations: How Can We Live in Harmony?

This unit focuses on race and ethnic relations, and the history and theory of race relations in Canada. It involves reading about the factors that influence the development of prejudice in individuals and society. It also gives definitions of terms related to race and ethnic relations. The unit leads to a lot of challenging discussion as you share the complex information from the reading.

The final project in this unit is to develop a mock-up of a public awareness campaign on the issues presented. You will be required to use the information from the unit and your own creativity to produce both a written report of your campaign and sample material from your campaign.

You should turn to the project description at the end of the unit regularly to see how much information and how many skills you need to help you complete it.

READING *You will use a variety of skills to read for information, and skim and scan academic text to get the most important information for your purposes. The readings are lengthy and complex.*

LISTENING *You will listen to a description of solutions to issues raised in the unit.*

WRITING *You will write short answers to tasks presented in the unit. As part of the awareness campaign, you will write a full report as well as campaign material.*

SPEAKING *You will discuss your opinions and information presented in the unit. You will talk and work together to create the final campaign.*

TO BEGIN, TURN THE PAGE AND START THINKING ABOUT AND DISCUSSING THE TOPIC IN GENERAL.

Introduction to the Topic

● SHARING BACKGROUND
  KNOWLEDGE
● PREDICTING

In a group of three, discuss the following questions. Use the spaces below to record any notes from your discussions. Then share your ideas with the class.

1. Without referring to a dictionary, define these terms:

   race _____

   _____

   ethnic group _____

   _____

   prejudice _____

   _____

   racism _____

   _____

2. Where does prejudice come from? What makes a person (or people) prejudiced, racist, or discriminatory?

3. Discuss some possible effects of prejudice on these two groups:
   a) the prejudiced people

   b) the targets of prejudice

4. What can be done to combat problems of prejudice, racism, and discrimination? Imagine a public campaign to fight these problems. What would such a campaign consist of?

TASK 2

Clarifying Terms

● FINDING DEFINITIONS
● GETTING THE MAIN IDEA
● SUMMARIZING

1. Go through the following reading, taken from a sociology textbook, and highlight the terms that are in **bold** or *italic* type.

2. Divide the highlighted terms among you in a group of three.

3. Take notes on each of the key terms assigned to you by answering these questions:

   a) How is the term defined?

   b) What examples are discussed in the text?

   c) What research is discussed in the text?

4. Compare your notes with those of classmates who have read the same information. Clear up any differences with reference to the text.

5. Discuss the information you have taken from the text with your original group. **Do not refer back to the reading during your discussion.**

6. On a separate sheet of paper, take notes on your discussion.

7. After you have finished your discussion, refer back to the text to clarify the information you have heard.

Race and minority group: social categories

Inherited features such as family surname and physical traits, such as skin color and hair texture, in themselves have no necessary consequences for behavior. Yet such identifying features often become *socially defined* as very significant. All individuals who have a particular characteristic, such as dark skin, may be seen by others as members of a single **social category**, which is defined as a collection of individuals all of whom share a single trait that is regarded as socially meaningful. The social meaning attached to racial or ethnic categories often includes the assignment of a rank within the hierarchy of society. This position is not necessarily subordinate; ethnicity is not always stigmatizing, nor always associated with oppression. It is quite possible for an ethnic group to occupy an elite or privileged status, as the British have historically done in the economic life of Quebec.

Frequently, however, racial or ethnic labels become criteria for assigning individuals or groups to subordinate positions within a social hierarchy. For this to occur, a labeling process takes place whereby individuals are socially identified as members of an ethnic or racial category, which in turn is defined as subordinate or inferior. Moghaddam and Taylor (1987) studied the effects of this labeling process on women who had immigrated to Canada from India. These women tended to perceive themselves as "women," "individuals," and "Canadian." But they felt they were perceived by most Canadians as "Indian," "women," "immigrants," "colored," and "South Asian"—labels associated with lower status in Canadian society.

Members of a social category may not have anything in common beyond their shared identifying features. However, if as a consequence of their treatment and position in society they become involved in social interaction with one another, and come to share values and a sense of identity and common interests, they may *become* a social group. This process of *ethnogenesis* has occurred among the First Nations of North America, who lived as separate and frequently warring groups, each with its own culture, until Europeans forced upon them a common label and identity. It was only because Columbus thought he had arrived in India that the label "Indians" was applied to aboriginal peoples of the Americas.

A **race** is not a social group, but an arbitrary social category, consisting of persons who share inherited physical characteristics such as skin color and facial features, characteristics charged with social meaning in some societies. An enormous amount of scientific evidence has invalidated notions that genetically separate races of human beings exist. A population may display a number of inherited physical features that tend to be less typical of other populations, but these features "are derived from a great reservoir of genes that is the common inheritance of all mankind" (Geipel, 1969: 3). In the words of Gould (1981: 323)

> … all modern human races probably split from a common ancestral stock only tens of thousands of years ago. A few outstanding traits of external appearance lead to our subjective judgement of important differences. But biologists have recently affirmed—as long suspected—that the overall genetic differences among human races are astonishingly small.

Moreover, research in genetics has established that the physical attributes that have been considered the markers of race, such as stature, skin and eye color, or hair texture, are inherited quite independently of one another and are not always found together. The so-called "races" thus can best be understood as social constructs defined by dominant groups in a society (Li, 1988: 23).

RACISM

Racism is an ideology that regards racial or ethnic categories as natural genetic groupings, and that attributes behavioral and psychological differences to the genetic nature of these groupings. Biological traits are used to label some human beings—invariably those belonging to categories other than the one doing the labeling—as inherently inferior, and therefore proper objects of exploitation and domination.

The concept of race stems primarily from the "scientific exploration of human origins." Incorporated into racist theories, the concept of race "purported to offer an explanation of and justification for the exploitation and subjugation of blacks by whites in terms of those origins. It is precisely for this reason that the term race is increasingly questioned as an appropriate analytic category in sociology just as it was earlier in biology" (Mason, 1988: 5-6).

Racist ideas and ideologies are even older than the scientific formulations of race, as old as history itself. During this century racist notions have been used to rationalize the oppression of aboriginal peoples, the Nazi extermination of Jews and Gypsies, and laws restricting the immigration of southern Europeans and Asian peoples to Canada and the United States.

Subordination of minorities

Racist ideologies as rationalizations for various forms of social, political, and economic oppression and control have contributed to keeping minority groups in disadvantaged economic and social positions, and to the destruction of entire peoples. A **minority group** is a social category that occupies a subordinate rank in a social hierarchy; such a group is accorded unequal treatment and excluded from full participation in the life of society. The term *minority* refers not to the size of the group—a minority may outnumber dominant groups, as in South Africa—but to its position in a context of power relationships. In post-Confederation Canada, Japanese, Chinese, Canadian Indians, Inuit, and blacks have suffered various restrictions on their freedom of access to employment, housing, education, and citizenship. The right to vote has at some time been denied to each of these groups.

In the modern world, extreme forms of social control have been used to subordinate minorities of all types. Such measures include *expulsion*, the forcible removal of a minority from its homeland—a fate suffered by Canada's First Nations during the settlement of the country, and by west coast Japanese Canadians during World War II. Soon after Canada declared war on Japan, all persons of Japanese origin living within one hundred miles of British Columbia's coastline, the majority of them Canadian citizens, were forcibly evacuated from their homes. They were stripped of their property and placed in "relocation centers" in Alberta, Ontario, and other provinces, where they lived in camps and worked as farm laborers. After the war most Japanese remaining in Canada did not return to their west coast communities, but remained dispersed in other areas.

The modern world has also seen instances of *annihilation* or *genocide*—the intentional massacre of peoples. The destruction of certain aboriginal groups as a result of the European conquest of the Americas, of European Jews and Gypsies by the Nazis, of Armenians in Turkey, and of Muslims in Bosnia-Herzegovina are but a few items in a catalogue of horrors (Chalk and Jonassohn, 1990).

Dominant groups frequently control and restrict the economic, social, and political participation of minorities by means of **discrimination**, the practice of denying to members of certain social categories opportunities that are generally available within the society. Discrimination may in some instances occur by legal means (*de jure*). For example, until 1960 an article of the Indian Act withheld the franchise from Indians in all provinces except Newfoundland. More common in Canada today is *de facto* or informal discrimination that occurs as a matter of common practice, often in violation of

the law, as in the case of a landlord who finds an excuse for refusing to rent an apartment to someone who is a member of a racial minority, in contravention of provincial human rights statutes.

Canadian evidence on the prevalence of discrimination against members of minority groups is accumulating. In a 1978-79 survey of Toronto ethnic groups, Breton (1990: 207-209) found that for a majority of West Indians (57 percent), discrimination against their group in employment was a serious concern. The same was true for 37 percent of Chinese, 33 percent of Portuguese, 20 percent of Italians, and 15 percent of Jews—and about the same proportions of the majority Canadian population agreed with these groups' perceptions of the discrimination they faced. Driedger and Mezoff (1981) found that two-thirds of Jewish high school students in their Winnipeg sample had experienced discrimination, in the form of verbal abuse, ethnic jokes, language ridicule, and other acts. Almost half the Polish-, Italian-, and French-origin students also reported these experiences. Approximately two-thirds of South Asian and West Indian respondents in a 1979 Toronto survey of social agency clients reported experiences of racial discrimination, primarily in housing and employment (Head, 1981: 72). The same proportion of women who had immigrated to Canada from India felt they had been badly treated in Canada because of their race (Moghaddam and Taylor, 1987: 134).

Systemic or **institutionalized discrimination** is a form of discrimination that occurs as a by-product of the ordinary functioning of bureaucratic institutions, rather than as a consequence of a deliberate policy or motive to discriminate. Systemic discrimination consists of patterns of institutional practices that perpetuate majority-group privilege and create disadvantage for minorities simply by conducting "business as usual." For example, by setting a rule that recruits must be at least five feet, ten inches tall, a police department may effectively exclude many Chinese and aboriginal applicants, since the average height of members of these groups is less than the requirement. By means of such arbitrary criteria that have no demonstrable relationship to job performance, privileged groups may control access to employment opportunities.

There is strong evidence that racial minorities in Canada face discrimination in employment, including wage discrimination. For example, in a study of 16 Canadian ethnic populations, Li (1988: 118-119) found that Chinese and blacks had higher educational levels than the national average. But when education, age, gender, and place of birth were statistically controlled, the average incomes of Chinese and blacks were the lowest of all the groups.

Research in Toronto has demonstrated the existence of direct discrimination by employers against black job applicants. Pairs of job applicants, matched in all respects except that one was black and the other white, applied for over 430 advertised jobs. The whites received three job offers for every one received by the black applicants (Henry and Ginzberg, 1985, 1993). Many other studies in Canada and the United States have shown how discriminatory employment practices restrict access to jobs, promotions, and equal pay for North American-born black and Asian minorities (Bielby 1987; Billingsley and Muszynski, 1985; Braddock and McPartland, 1987; Duleep and Sandlers, 1992). Analyses of data for Toronto (Reitz, 1990: 151) and Canada (Boyd, 1993; Li, 1992) demonstrate that when education and other characteristics are taken into account, minority women face even more income disadvantage than minority men in the workplace. Women who are members of minority groups, then, are doubly disadvantaged in employment (Malveaux and Wallace, 1987; Neallani, 1992).

Discrimination in employment is reinforced in some societies by the practice of segregation on the basis of minority status. **Segregation** is a form of social control whereby physical distance is maintained in order to insure social distance from groups with whom contact is not wanted. Segregation involves the exclusion of ethnic, racial, or other minorities from the facilities, residential space, or institutions used by dominant groups.

Under an elaborate system of segregation in South Africa known as *apartheid*, or apartness, blacks generally were forbidden by law to enter the residential neighborhoods, workplaces, public buildings, or recreational facilities used by whites, and restricted to inferior facilities provided for blacks only. In response to organized resistance to apartheid by blacks in southern Africa, and to international pressure, the South African government committed itself to ending the system of apartheid. The first elections in which South African blacks had the right to vote took place in April, 1994. Nelson Mandela became South Africa's first black president. It is likely that under Mandela segregation will be abolished and discrimination generally will continue to diminish.

In the southern United States, from the late nineteenth century until the early 1960s, an elaborate system of *de jure* racial discrimination, segregation, and oppression known as "Jim Crow" prevailed. Blacks were legally forbidden to use public facilities such as schools and universities, recreational facilities, restrooms, water fountains, and bus seats designated for whites. They were not served in restaurants or stores catering to whites. In general they were denied equal status in their contact with whites and were excluded from most employment opportunities.

As a consequence of the massive institutional changes resulting from the civil rights movement, U.S. blacks and whites increasingly meet in the public sphere. However, both economic inequality and residential segregation have remained entrenched, despite legislation at all levels of government that forbids discrimination in housing throughout the United States. Because of segregated residential patterns and income disadvantages, over 75 percent of black students in Illinois, New York, Michigan, California, and Mississippi attend segregated schools (Hacker, 1992: 163).

Large black residential ghettos like those of U.S. cities are infrequent in Canada, except in Nova Scotia, although ghettos of Native peoples occur and may be expanding as their urbanization proceeds (Frideres, 1983). However, residential separation among ethnic and racial groups is high and persistent in Canadian cities, even when socioeconomic status is taken into account (Kalbach, 1990; Balakrishnan, 1982). In Canada, indexes of residential segregation are highest for the Jewish and Portuguese populations and moderate for the black, Chinese, Hungarian, Russian, and Italian groups (Kalbach, 1990: 98). In Toronto, the Chinese and black populations show a pattern of scattered pockets of concentration (Kalbach, 1990: 130). Research suggests that people's desire to live near others of the same background, discrimination, and poverty may all be causal factors in ethnic and racial residential separation (Agócs, 1979).

Explaining discrimination

In search of explanations for the existence of discrimination against minority groups in modern societies, social scientists have studied various kinds of influences. Before the 1960s there was much interest in the role of ideas and beliefs in motivating discriminatory acts against minority group members. Of special importance was the concept of **prejudice**, an attitude that prejudges individuals because of characteristics assumed to be shared by all members of their group. Those characteristics may be conceptualized as **stereotypes**—mental images that exaggerate what are usually perceived to be undesirable traits of typical members of a group, and are applied to all of its members. A stereotype is a premature or inaccurate generalization about members of a group that gets in the way of knowing these persons as individuals. Further, stereotypes may provide a rationalization for unequal treatment.

Basic Sociology: A Canadian Introduction, Fifth Edition, James J. Teevan, W. E. Hewitt, © 1995. Used by permission of Prentice Hall Canada Inc.

T A S K 3

Getting Background Information About the Topic

● FOLLOWING CHRONOLOGICAL STRUCTURE OF INFORMATION IN A TEXT
● GETTING THE MAIN IDEA
● SUMMARIZING

Follow the steps below in order to summarize the information in this reading, from a sociology textbook, which is organized chronologically.

1. Scan the first sentence of each paragraph. In a small group, create a diagram on a separate sheet of paper to illustrate the chronological (time-related) structure of this reading. For example, you could consider using a tree, boxes, circles, or a line.

2. Divide the paragraphs among you in your small group. Read the paragraphs assigned to you. Enter point-form notes in the appropriate place or places on your diagram.

3. Prepare to explain the information that you have learned. Keep in mind that you will **not** have access to your notes or the text when you explain.

4. Share your information as a group, helping each other to fill in the diagrams you created. **Do not refer back to your notes or the reading itself.**

5. Now take a few minutes to review the information in this text by answering the questions below.

    a) What are the most important developments in the history of Canada's multicultural society? Write them here in point-form:

    b) Referring only to your notes and using a separate sheet of paper, write a brief summary of the most important developments, one paragraph per main idea.

It is inaccurate to think of Canadian society as nothing but two unified ethnic blocs in confrontation, complex as the implications of such an image may be. A history of massive immigration has created a much more complex pluralism in Canada, one marked by a high degree of ethnic and class diversity. According to official figures, roughly twelve and a half million foreign-born people came to Canada between 1851 and 1991.

The first decade of the twentieth century was a peak period of net immigration into Canada. It is true that immigration had already reached a rather high level in the late nineteenth century, when the building of the Canadian Pacific Railway and the opening of the west attracted a wave of settlers from Britain and the United States. However, immigrants to Canada at that time were outnumbered by Canadians immigrating to the United States, mainly because many French Canadians found it necessary to leave the overpopulated farms and job-poor villages of Quebec to work in the textile factories of New England.

In the first decade of this century the economy and society of Canada were still largely agrarian, and government policy was oriented toward agricultural development. The vast prairie lands had yet to come under the plow, and the Canadian government sought to promote immigration to "settle the empty west with producing farmers," in the words of Clifford Sifton, then Minister of the Interior and architect of Canada's immigration policy in the early twentieth century (Royal Commission on Bilingualism and Biculturalism, IV: 22). Government sponsorship of recruitment and transportation for immigrant peasants and farmers from Europe and the United States and the availability of free land combined to double the foreign-born population of the prairies from 1901 to 1911. The majority of immigrants in those years, as in earlier decades, came from Great Britain and the United States. While many of the British immigrants, like the Irish settlers of the nineteenth century, gravitated toward the industrial cities, large numbers of the Americans, among them people of German, Polish, Danish, and various other ethnic backgrounds, joined the stream of new farmers to the prairies. At the same time the first heavy wave of immigrants came from central and eastern Europe; among those were Ukrainians, Poles, Hungarians, and Russians.

Early twentieth-century rural ethnic settlements in Manitoba, Saskatchewan, and Alberta frequently took the form of isolated and homogeneous communities, described by Dawson in a classic study called *Group Settlement: Ethnic Communities in Western Canada* (1936). The bloc settlements of such groups as Doukhobors, Mennonites, German Catholics, Mormons, and French Canadians constituted "culture islands," each occupying a territorial base set off from surrounding populations by distinctive language, institutions, and religious or national identity. They were relatively successful as settlers because of their group settlement patterns and the cooperative nature of their social organization, which differed from the myth of the individualistic pioneer homesteader.

The era of the farmer-immigrant was a relatively brief one in Canada's history, for the predominant pattern of immigrant settlement has long been urban. As early as 1921, the first year for which data are available, 56 percent of Canada's foreign-born were living in urban areas, compared with only 48 percent of the Canadian-born. The transformation of Canada from an agrarian to an urban industrial society was already well underway at that time, and opportunities for industrial employment in the growing cities attracted both farm-reared Canadians and immigrants. In addition, modernization was transforming the countryside and shutting off opportunities in farming. Farms were growing in size and efficiency, and because of mechanization, fewer hands were needed to produce more food, while greater capital investments were required for successful farm operation. The isolated immigrant farmer, settled on marginal farmland, had difficulty competing, and the rate of failures among homesteaders was high. In cities like Toronto, Montreal, and Hamilton, therefore, unsuccessful farmers—many of them immigrants—joined the ranks of new arrivals from Europe and Canadian migrants from the overpopulated farms of Quebec, Nova Scotia, New Brunswick, and Ontario.

An era of accelerated urbanization and a second peak period of immigration followed World War II. Before the war, about 54 percent of Canada's total population and 60 percent of its foreign-born were urban dwellers, but by 1971 the proportions had reached 76 percent of all Canadians and 88 percent of immigrants (Kalbach, 1978: 99). Cityward migration of Canadians, as well as immigration, contributed to the growing ethnic diversity of the cities during the postwar years. Settlements of blacks from rural Nova Scotia took shape in Montreal; French Canadians from the farms and rural villages of Quebec became the miners and mill workers of Sudbury; Newfoundlanders put down roots in Hamilton; and Native peoples settled in Winnipeg and Regina.

The heavy influx of new immigrants during the years since 1945 also contributed to urban ethnic diversity, since the vast majority of these immigrants have settled in the seven largest metropolitan areas of

Canada. For example, in 1991, 38 percent of the population of metropolitan Toronto and 30 percent of Vancouver residents were born outside Canada. Immigrants tend to gravitate toward destinations that offer economic opportunity. In an urban industrial society, job opportunities are most plentiful in the largest cities, and the effects of chain migration are also seen in the congregation of immigrants there. By 1991, 57 percent of all immigrants to Canada were living in Toronto, Montreal, and Vancouver, compared with 26 percent of the Canadian-born population, according to the census (Statistics Canada, 1993, *1991 Census of Canada, Immigration and Citizenship: The Nation*, Catalogue No. 93-316, Table 5).

Since World War II, the predominance of British immigrants has given way to a broader mix of peoples. While the United Kingdom and the United States have continued to contribute large numbers of immigrants, Chinese, Indians, Italians, Dutch, Vietnamese, Poles, Portuguese, and people from the Caribbean, the Philippines, and the African and South American continents have joined them. Over 300 000 people have come to Canada as refugees since World War II, having been displaced by revolutions and political oppression in their homelands. In the 1980s, on average, slightly less than one-fifth of immigrants claimed refugee status (Badets, 1989). With the refocusing of immigration policy in the 1970s to emphasize occupational skills, educational qualifications, demands of the economy, family reunification, and refugee criteria instead of national origin, the immigrant population has become increasingly heterogeneous and representative of third-world countries. Before 1978, immigrants originating in Europe made up 70 percent of newcomers to Canada, but since that time have made up less than 30 percent of immigrants, while people born in Asia have constituted 40 percent of immigrants since 1978 (Badets, 1989).

Richmond (1967) showed postwar immigration to be marked by fluidity as well as by ethnic diversity. It is quite common today for people to leave their native countries to seek temporary or permanent work or specialized training in another country. Richmond found that almost a fourth of all postwar immigrants to Canada came with the intention of returning to their homelands. Surprisingly, immigrants from countries most similar to Canada, such as Britain or the U.S., are most likely to go back to their home countries. Those who have to make the most fundamental changes in their lives are the immigrants most likely to remain in Canada and to be satisfied residents of their new country. Thus, immigrants from Italy, Greece, or Portugal, who must learn a new language and who frequently face unpleasant working conditions and culture shock, are more inclined to stay in Canada and become citizens than are British or American immigrants, who on average enjoy a far higher occupational status and income during their early years in Canada (Satzewich and Li, 1987: 235-237). A survey of "family class" immigrants found, moreover, that while those from developing countries face barriers in the workplace, they rarely receive economic support from the government. They are more likely to receive assistance from relatives and to seek employment. Many become entrepreneurs who in turn create jobs for others in Canada (Samuel, 1988).

Basic Sociology: A Canadian Introduction, Fifth Edition, James J. Teevan, W. E. Hewitt, © 1995. Used by permission of Prentice Hall Canada Inc.

TASK

Getting In-depth Background Information About the Topic

- READING FOR A PURPOSE
- GETTING THE MAIN IDEA
- SUMMARIZING
- EVALUATING

PERSPECTIVES ON CANADIAN RACE AND ETHNIC RELATIONS

Follow the steps below to get information from this academic text and to determine what the future may hold for ethnic and race relations in Canada.

1. Divide the three perspectives in this reading among you in a group of three.

2. Read the perspective assigned to you and take notes on a separate sheet of paper.

3. Form a group with students who have read the same information. Discuss your notes and clarify differences by referring back to the text.

4. Study your notes and prepare to discuss them without re-ferring back to the reading.

5. Using only your notes, and without referring back to the original text, explain the perspective to your group members.

6. As a group, try to reach agreement on an answer to this question:

   Which perspective has the most positive implications for public policy in Canada?

   Justify your decision with reference to the text.

7. Form new groups with members from other original groups. Explain your group's answer to the question. Do you agree or disagree? Refer to the information in the text to justify the points you make.

| READING | PERSPECTIVES ON CANADIAN RACE AND ETHNIC RELATIONS |

We now turn our attention to three dominant perspectives on inter-group relations within a pluralistic society—assimilationism, two-category perspectives, and pluralism. Each perspective functions in two ways at the same time. First, each describes a social reality, and second, each contains suggestions about the future of ethnic and race relations, and as a result, has implications for social policy.

Assimilationism

The interpretation of ethnic group relations that dominated North American thought for at least the first half of the twentieth century was assimilationism—the view that ethnic diversity gradually and in-evitably declines as ethnic group members are integrated or absorbed into the general population of the society. Ethnic groups are viewed as transitory rather than central and enduring features of modern society. This is partly because of the assumed irrele-vance of ethnic diversity to the political, social, and economic life of modern industrial society, which is viewed as rational, achievement-oriented, bureau-cratically organized, and international in scope. Attachments of sentiment, ascription, kinship, com-munity, and shared culture, which are fundamental to ethnic identity, are seen as survivals of an earlier stage of societal development and out of place in the modern age. This view of ethnicity is usually held by functionalists, but it could be argued that most of the great sociological theorists, from Marx to Weber to Durkheim, have reflected such a perception.

Assimilation is the process of becoming part of the larger surrounding society and culture by becom-ing more and more like the dominant group, so that in time Polish Canadians, for example, would be in-distinguishable from the British or French Canadians with whom they live. As a group they are unique only while they are relatively recent arrivals. In time they will improve their social and economic position and disappear into the great melting pot, in which various ethnic groups and cultures blend into a sin-gle culture and society.

The melting pot image has been a prominent fea-ture of national identity in the United States, but as-similationism as a description and social ideal has also had its adherents in Canada (e.g., Porter, 1980). Assimilationist assumptions were reflected in official policy toward immigrants and ethnic groups before World War II. The preference for British immigrants and the existence of severe restrictions on the immi-gration of racially and culturally different peoples have already been mentioned. These restrictions were based, in part, on the assumption that those peoples who are most similar to the dominant Canadian pop-ulation—the British—would most readily adapt to life in Canada, cause fewest problems for the domi-nant group, and ultimately assimilate.

Assimilationist thinkers generally hold liberal, in-dividualistic values, and assume that it is only through individual achievement that upward mobil-ity in the social hierarchy can occur. They further assume that maintaining one's ethnic culture and languages will hinder upward mobility because it reduces acceptance of the ethnic group member by the majority group. Thus, ethnic group members must accept a trade-off: giving up their ethnicity in return for social acceptance, improved status, and a good standard of living.

In the United States assimilationism as a realistic description of American society has been called into question by research documenting the persistence of ethnic differences and racial inequality (e.g., McCready, 1983). The notion that the assimilationist perspective provides a useful interpretation of the realities of ethnic group relations is not as widely held in Canada, where the image of the mosaic has long been a national symbol of its ethnic diversity. As discussed previously, patterns of ethnic and especially racial inequality remain entrenched both for men and for women, even when level of education is controlled. The Canadian mosaic continues to be a vertical one.

As a social goal and guide to policy, assimilationism has also been subjected to damaging criticism. The assimilationist perspective suggests that, if the goal is equality of opportunity for all, then public institutions must be universalistic rather than particularistic. That is, institutions must apply the same set of rules to every individual in the same way, "regardless of race, religion, or national origin." They cannot treat members of some groups one way and members of other groups another. Groups, then, are officially ignored, and only the claims of individuals are recognized by assimilationist theorists. It is assumed that in order to be equal, people must all be alike, and that equality means treating everyone alike, regardless of their differences.

It had become apparent by the 1960s that the condition of blacks and Native peoples as groups was not improving through the process of social mobility whereby individuals play by the universalistic rules of the game. The goal of bringing these groups into the mainstream of American and Canadian societies has seemed farther and farther away as census data chart the continuing gap between the incomes and unemployment rates of blacks and Natives, on the one hand, and the rest of the population on the other. The historical legacy of slavery, colonialism, discrimination, and cultural destruction weighs heavily upon present generations.

Many thoughtful observers in academic and public life concluded that extraordinary measures have to be taken to overcome the barriers to assimilation and integration that result from long-standing patterns of discrimination and disadvantage. The application of universalistic rules and standards is resulting in what we earlier called systemic or institutionalized discrimination. Inequality is built into the occupational structure, and many minority group members are not even getting to the starting gate in the race for advancement. The rules of the game are not fair to all, since they were established by the majority, and serve to maintain their position of privilege. It follows that the rules must be changed in order to remove those barriers that have excluded minorities from access to jobs, promotions, and career advancement.

Employment equity, which became permissible under Canadian federal law in 1977, is a broad strategy for change in the policies, practices, and culture of the workplace (Agócs, Burr, and Somerset, 1992). Its objectives are to increase the representation of disadvantaged groups at all levels of the occupational structure, to remove barriers to their career advancement, and to create a workplace culture free of discrimination. In Canada at the present time, the designated employment equity groups are Native peoples, visible minorities, women, and people with disabilities.

In 1983 employment equity became mandatory in the federal public service, and since 1986 employers who sell goods or services to the federal government have been required to implement employment equity programs. Federally regulated employers and crown corporations are required by law to report annually on the representation of designated group members in their work force, but there are no sanctions if they fail to implement employment equity programs. Existing federal legislation and regulations are weak, and many employers are not covered. Hence it is not surprising that there has been little evidence of consistent improvement in the position of racial minorities, Native peoples, women, and persons with disabilities in the workplace (Agócs, Burr, and Somerset, 1992). Many who are concerned about persisting patterns of racial and gender inequality in Canadian society have advocated a more serious commitment to employment equity by employers and by governments, and more attention to effective means of working toward change in the workplace.

Two-category perspectives

Scholars who theorize a two-category system of race relations in North America have argued that the assimilationist perspective describes whites only. Blacks and Native peoples are in a separate category; they have not been part of the melting pot because of the persistence of racism in society, which has its roots in the historical experiences of slavery and colonialism. They are viewed as minority groups who continue to occupy a disadvantaged position in a society dominated by whites, who constitute a single homogeneous social category. Rioux (1978b) has argued that the Québécois are also a minority group in this sense, one whose destiny is unique because of its historical position as a people conquered, colonized, and dominated by the British.

Two-category perspectives on race relations are pluralistic in the sense that they view society not as a single body but as two separate collectivities in conflict. These two distinct social categories are hierarchically ranked, and bound together in a relationship of dominance and subordination within a single society and culture.

Examining several nineteenth- and twentieth-century societies in which the institutions of slavery and colonialism were integral parts of the development of modern capitalism, Van den Berghe (1967) developed a two-category theory of relationships between the races. According to him liberal democratic societies such as the United States face the dilemma of reconciling their ideals of liberty and equality with their oppression of black slaves and their extermination of Native peoples. Van den Berghe reasoned that this reconciliation was accomplished ideologically by dividing humanity into two categories—"the civilized" (the human beings) and the "savages" (the inferior beings whose humanity was denied). The application of egalitarian and democratic ideas was restricted to those defined as "the civilized," that is, the dominant white group. The result in countries such as the United States and South Africa is what Van den Berghe called a "Herrenvolk democracy"—a system that was "democratic for the master race but tyrannical for the subordinate groups" (Van den Berghe, 1967: 18).

Could such a harsh image apply in any way to Canadian reality? Although slavery did not become entrenched in Canada, it did thrive until the passage of the Emancipation Act by the British Parliament in 1833. Blacks have been subject to discrimination not only under Canadian immigration law, but also in employment, public accommodations, housing, and education. Segregated black schools existed in Ontario and Nova Scotia until the mid-1960s (Krauter and Davis, 1978: 50). However, an all-encompassing system of *de jure* racial segregation like that of the southern United States never became established in Canada. The image of a distinct, racially defined social category standing in a relationship of legalized subordination to whites apparently does not apply to blacks in Canada in the same way that it did in the United States.

However, Canada is not without its own race-relations dilemma. The reserve system has long been the principal instrument of Canadian policy toward the First Nations. It is a policy that has treated the various Indian peoples as a single social category with "special status" under the law, excluded from the larger society yet dependent upon that society, hence subordinate to it. While keeping Indians socially, politically, and economically separate and subordinate, the reserve system and the Indian Act have been instruments of acculturation to the religions, languages, values, and traditions of the larger society, and of the destruction of First Nations' cultures and social structures.

The First Nations are not merely one of the many ethnic groups in the Canadian mosaic. Because of their aboriginal rights, and because of the history of colonialism to which Native peoples have uniquely been subjected, they are fundamentally different from other groups, and require recognition as autonomous peoples equal in status to the English and French. As such, the First Nations are entitled to control over their ancestral lands, self-determination, and the right to deal collectively with the government of Canada—a right implied in the government's traditional practice of making treaty agreements with aboriginal peoples as nations. Many bands and Native organizations such as the Assembly of First Nations (representing status Indians), the Native Council of Canada (representing Métis and non-status Indians), and the Inuit Tapirisat have been negotiating for many years with the government of Canada and initiating court actions in attempts to gain self-government and ownership of lands traditionally occupied and used by aboriginal peoples, and never ceded under treaties. In pressing their claims, First Nations are attempting to ensure the survival of their peoples and cultures as distinct entities, and to improve their standard of living and access to opportunity for succeeding generations.

This perspective challenges the assimilationist assumption, explicit in federal policy since Confederation, that First Nations should be absorbed into the larger society. The need to implement an alternative to the reserve system, and the movement toward self-government by aboriginal peoples, present a major policy dilemma for Canada's pluralistic society.

Pluralism

During this generation, the worldwide rise of nationalistic movements has shaken loose historic accommodations between dominant and subordinate ethnic and racial groups, not only in Canada and the United States but also in many parts of Africa, Europe, Asia, and even the former Soviet Union. Ethnic and aboriginal communities across Canada have sought public recognition of their distinctive aspirations and ways of life, and racial minorities have demanded an end to discrimination. Ethnic and racial diversity are very much a part of our contemporary society, and "assimilation" seems as far away as it ever has. From Québécois, First Nations, Jews, Chinese, Haitians, and many other groups come the questions: Can't we all enjoy equal opportunities as members of one society while maintaining our differences, our identities, and our communities? Can we not coexist as equals within a single society, even though we do not all look the same, or share the same values and culture?

Pluralism, the view that ethnic diversity and conflict remain a central feature of contemporary societies and that ethnicity continues to be an important aspect of individual identity and group behavior, has been widely accepted in the post-World War II era.

The image of the ethnic mosaic has become integral to Canadian national identity, and a feature said to distinguish Canadian from American values and culture. It is generally understood today that "Canadian culture" itself is not a homogeneous whole, but an intricate tapestry of many hues woven from the strands of many ethnic and regional subcultures.

Since Canada is a pluralistic society, both assimilation and ethnic and racial differentiation are going on at the same time. While in some respects Canada's ethnic groups become more alike as time passes, in many ways their influence brings an increasing diversity to the cultural, social, and political life shared by all Canadians. For example, immigrants, by becoming citizens and voting, may show signs of assimilation. Yet in local elections they may support candidates who represent their own ethnic groups' interests, thus bringing diversity to the political spectrum.

In fact, many pluralists contend that ethnic group members make progress and improve their positions in the social hierarchy not by individual achievement and dissociation from their roots, as assimilationists would argue, but by group efforts, using ethnic solidarity as a resource. It is collective action that benefits the group, and thereby its individual members. When members of an ethnic community vote in a bloc they force the political system to recognize and respond to their concerns. When relatives pool their resources to start a business, they not only provide jobs for their kin, but also contribute to the economic life of their community. When members of the community patronize ethnic businesses, they strengthen the community's overall business climate. When successful ethnic businesspeople are able to assist their children to attend university, they help to provide the community's next generation of leaders. In all of these examples it is the collective action of the community, rather than the efforts of isolated individuals to achieve upward mobility, that brings progress to members of the group.

A study of Iranians in Montreal suggests that different members of the same ethnic group adopt varied strategies in integrating into Canadian society. In the study, those immigrants who chose a strategy of ethnic cultural maintenance were more likely to belong to Iranian organizations and to endorse collective means of getting ahead. Those who agreed with an assimilationist strategy tended not to belong to Iranian organizations and to have an individualistic view of mobility. Both groups had a high level of confidence in their ability to do well in Canada (Moghaddam, Taylor, and Lalonde, 1987). Many studies (e.g., Breton et al., 1990) have provided evidence that ethnic groups, as well as individuals, adopt a variety of different approaches as they integrate into Canadian society and improve their socio-economic position, while retaining varying degrees of ethnic identity and community solidarity.

The increasing heterogeneity of Canada's population, the growing numerical strength and voting power of ethnic groups, and the acceptance of a collectivist strategy have coincided with a shift away from the official image of Canada as a bicultural country toward a recognition of it as multicultural. In 1971 Prime Minister Trudeau, with the support of all political parties, announced a policy of "multiculturalism within a bilingual framework," under which federal recognition and support would be extended to the various ethnic groups that constitute the Canadian mosaic (Government of Canada, 1971). The Multiculturalism Act of 1988 affirms the government's commitment to the preservation and appreciation of cultural diversity, and to promoting the full and equal participation of individuals and communities in all aspects of Canadian society (Elliott and Fleras, 1990). However, critics (e.g., Li, 1988) have noted a lack of results and questioned the government's real commitment to these principles.

The institutions of Canadian society have begun to grapple with the fact that ethnicity is not just an individual trait, but a fundamental characteristic of the social system as a whole. The specific implications of this fact are far-reaching and complex. They include questions about whether groups should have rights to political representation and to educational and government services, not just in French and English, but in any language now spoken in Canada. Perhaps most important, Canadian institutions now face the challenge of assisting Canadians to live in harmony and mutual respect in a society in which ethnic and racial diversity will continue to grow.

PLURALISTIC SOCIETIES IN THE CONTEMPORARY WORLD

Following the end of World War II, many hoped that the era of nationalist and ethnic conflict was at an end. Two horrifying world wars had shown the destructive potential of nationalism. A worldwide system of political and military alliances and economic cooperation was taking shape, and the newly created United Nations held out the promise of one world. Visionary social thinkers nurtured dreams of a new cosmopolitan world order.

This hope was not to be realized, however, for new divisive and disruptive forces soon appeared, and old unresolved tensions resurfaced; new nations splintered off, old nations were swallowed up in conquest; new ethnic groups made themselves heard, while ancient ones made new demands. Since then, ethnic and racial conflict has grown and spread until its influence on world events sometimes overshadows that of class conflict.

In Europe, Serbs, Croats, and Muslims in Bosnia-Herzegovina have been engulfed in a terrifying cycle of killing and "ethnic cleansing." The independence movements of Tamils in Sri Lanka, Kurds in Iraq, and Sikhs in India are only a few examples of current struggles of ethnic minorities for self-determination. The dramatic and unexpected collapse of the Union of Soviet Socialist Republics in 1989 can be viewed, in part, as a result of unresolved ethnic tensions and nationalistic aspirations long constrained by a repressive imperialistic state. In Northern Ireland children trade Molotov cocktails in the endless exchange of terrorist acts between Catholics and Protestants. South Africans continue to face the daunting challenge of emerging from a history of racism, repression, and violence into a new era of political, economic, and social democracy and racial equality.

The issues of racial and ethnic inequality in the world continue to command our attention and response. The roll call of ethnic and racial strife seems endless and leaves no corner of the world untouched. The daily newspapers are full of tensions between groups who are in conflict because of differences in race, national origin, religion, or language. It appears that ethnic conflict and demands for autonomy, rather than integration and assimilation, are the conditions of modern life. Some racial and ethnic conflicts seem rooted in the struggles of colonized or conquered peoples for liberation or self-determination. Others express the need of modern people for meaning, identity, autonomy, and a sense of belonging and community in a world increasingly dominated by remote, large-scale, bureaucratic organizations. Both the need for liberation and the need to belong will continue to challenge future generations in Canada and throughout the world.

Basic Sociology: A Canadian Introduction, Fifth Edition, James J. Teevan, W. E. Hewitt, © 1995. Used by permission of Prentice Hall Canada Inc.

TASK 5

More In-depth Information

- USING SURVEYING AND QUESTIONING TO GET INFORMATION FROM TEXT
- GETTING THE MAIN IDEA
- SUMMARIZING
- EVALUATING

ACQUISITION OF PREJUDICE

Follow the steps below to get a thorough knowledge of the information in this academic reading.

1. **Survey** the text, observing the headings, subheadings, and the first sentence of each paragraph.

2. For each item that you observed in step 1 above, **formulate a question**. For example, for the heading "Role of the Parents," a question might be, "What is the role of parents in the acquisition of prejudice?" Write your questions on a separate sheet of paper, leaving plenty of space after each one.

3. Now **read** the text to answer the questions that you have created. Take notes on the relevant information.

4. **Review** the information by discussing it with a partner. Clear up any differences you have about the information.

5. On a separate sheet of paper, **summarize** the information by rewriting it without looking at the text again. You may use your notes. You will be given a limited time to complete this step.

6. Share your summary with a partner. Which factors related to the acquisition of prejudice do you feel are the most important? List them here:

Innate or acquired

Hebb and Thompson (1968) have described incidents which suggested to them that the higher animals—chimpanzees and human beings—have an inherent fear of the unfamiliar and unusual. If Hebb is correct, though, as yet, there is no strong empirical support for his contention, it would be reasonable to argue that this tendency could form the basis for the development of prejudice, which is directed toward people perceived as being in some way different. It is generally agreed that people are anxious or fearful in situations which they do not understand. Perhaps the negative emotions directed at the members of an out-group have their roots in the spontaneous arousal generated by a new or novel stimulus.

It has been shown that infants as young as three months of age are able to distinguish between the face of their mother and that of a stranger. Although at this age their reactions to the unfamiliar stimulus do not show signs of avoidance or fear, by about the age of nine months, aversive reactions often do appear, frequently to the mother's embarrassment when, for instance, the unfamiliar stimulus is the child's grandmother.

It is also possible that a finding first reported by Zajonc (1968a) can be used to support Hebb's view. Zajonc demonstrated that there is a relationship between the frequency of occurrence of an event, or the number of times an individual is exposed to a stimulus, and the extent to which the stimulus is subsequently found to be attractive. This occurs in the absence of any additional information or interaction. Initially it was thought that this "mere exposure" effect happened regardless of whether a subject's initial attitude toward the stimulus was negative, positive, or neutral but later research (Perlman and Oskamp, 1971) indicates that only positive or neutral stimuli are enhanced. The evaluation of negative stimuli is not only unlikely to improve, but may deteriorate further.

Whether, in fact, there are inherent predispositions which could form the primitive rudiments of prejudice remains to be confirmed. There is, however, little doubt concerning the importance of *learning* in the development of prejudice. The first setting in which this learning takes place is the home.

Learning

ROLE OF THE PARENTS   Parents have a powerful influence, not only because they play a role in what the child learns from day to day, but because this learning forms the foundation for all subsequent experience, both familial and extra-familial. In order for prejudicial attitudes to be acquired, children must first become "racially aware." That is, they must be able to distinguish themselves from others who are, in some way, different. Children are aware of different ethnic groups by the age of four or five (Aboud, 1988). Racial awareness has been shown to be present in children as young as three years of age and, in one study, it was found that 25 percent of the four-year-old children observed were already expressing strong race-related values (Goodman, 1964).

Aboud (1988) argues for a three-stage process of prejudice acquisition. In the early years, she says that ethnic attitudes are based on emotions and needs. The child then moves on to a second stage in which perception is dominant. At this stage, perception of the child's own appearance and another's appearance and behaviour may influence attitudes. The third, cognitive, stage is reached by the age of seven or eight. It is at this point that three important ethnic cognitions are established. These are:

(1) Members of an ethnic group have psychological as well as physical and behavioural characteristics.
(2) There may be variations in skin colour or clothing among members of the same ethnic group (cognitive constancy).
(3) Different attributes can exist in two people who are ethnically the same, and the same attribute can exist in two people who are ethnically different (cognitive flexibility).

Aboud points out that more tolerant children are likely to be more flexible in their ethnic relations.

A number of the steps in this sequence occur before the child's horizons have expanded much beyond the home. In these early years, the parents have sole control over the child's rewards and punishments. During the waking hours one or the other of them is in almost continuous contact with the child so that there are many opportunities for habits of thought and action to be acquired.

It should be noted that in increasing numbers, children are being placed in daycare facilities. They may spend as much or even more time with an employee of the daycare centre as with their parents. These employees also may have a significant influence on attitude development.

Social learning can occur in a number of ways and under a variety of conditions. Three types of learning which are usually distinguished are: instrumental conditioning, classical conditioning, and modelling. Each has different implications for the acquisition of prejudice.

INSTRUMENTAL CONDITIONING One of the basic principles of instrumental (or operant) learning is that any behaviour or response which is followed by a reinforcement will be strengthened, that is, the probability that the response will occur again will be increased. Most of the reinforcements associated with the acquisition of prejudice are likely to be verbal or non-verbal indications of approval. For example, if a child says, "Those people are dirty," and the mother smiles and responds positively, then the child is likely to repeat this remark, make it part of his or her belief system and also generalize it to other similar-looking people.

CLASSICAL CONDITIONING Since Pavlov's first experiments with his salivating dogs, the classical conditioning paradigm has become part of almost everyone's psychological repertoire. In the original situation, an unconditioned stimulus (UCS), food, was used to elicit salivation in a dog. This UCS was then paired for a number of trials with the sound of a bell, the conditioned stimulus (CS). Subsequently, it was found that the CS, in the absence of the UCS, elicited salivation. This process is illustrated in the figure below.

A similar process may account for at least some portion of the emotional or evaluative aspect of prejudice. For example, suppose a White child is playing with an East Indian child and the White child's mother, noticing this interaction, rushes out, yells at her child to stop, slaps her, and drags her into the house. This treatment is the unconditioned stimulus which arouses hostility, fear, and anxiety in the child. The conditioned stimulus is the other, East Indian, child. If this situation is sufficiently traumatic and is repeated either with the same child or with other out-group children, ultimately the sight or presence of such a conditioned stimulus will be sufficient to elicit at least some portion of the negative feelings which were aroused in the original situation. This process is illustrated in the figure on the next page.

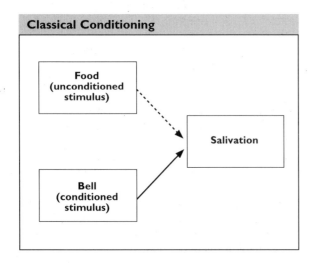

Classical Conditioning

MODELLING Not all learning involves the active intervention of a rewarding or punishing agent. Often a child will exhibit behaviour or express ideas which have not been deliberately taught but which have been observed being performed by others. Models, usually individuals with whom the child identifies, e.g., parents or teachers, have been shown to be highly effective in teaching attitudes and prejudice (Bandura, 1965). The process is both subtle and insidious because the child is not a direct participant in the event and the model may not be aware of the information that is being transmitted or its effect. It also should be kept in mind that what the model *does not do* may be just as important as what the model does do. Thus, avoiding an Asian cashier in a supermarket or commenting that "you should always count your change after those people wait on you" may each communicate similar information to the observing child.

THE PREJUDICED PERSONALITY Parents who have authoritarian traits teach their children that status is very important. These parents typically use harsh punishment, do not tolerate any hostility or aggression by the child toward them, act in a cold and impersonal manner, and withdraw love in order to maintain "proper" behaviour. Thus the child is forced to submit without question to his or her superiors and to suppress the hostility which is aroused naturally under these frustrating conditions. At the same time, by defining what is different as inferior, the parents give the child an acceptable outlet for pent-up feelings—out-groups. They also teach their children that the world is a dangerous place, thereby setting the stage for fear based on feelings of vulnerability (Altemeyer, 1988).

These individuals, identified as having an *authoritarian personality*, also are likely to be prejudiced and ethnocentric. In this case, prejudice is incorporated in a belief and value system which forms a personality pattern first identified by Adorno, Frenkel-Brunswick, Levinson and Sanford (1950). Adorno and his colleagues were initially interested in anti-Semitism but later broadened their perspective to include attitudes toward ethnic groups in general. As part of their study, they constructed a number of scales to measure anti-Semitic attitudes, ethnocentrism and authoritarianism. However, it was the concept of the "authoritarian personality" which attracted the most attention and which stimulated numerous subsequent research projects (e.g., Christie and Jahoda, 1954; Cherry and Byrne, 1977). It was found that individuals who can be characterized as authoritarian are likely to be prejudiced and to have a rigid personality in which the world is perceived in categorical black/white, superior/inferior, us/them terms.

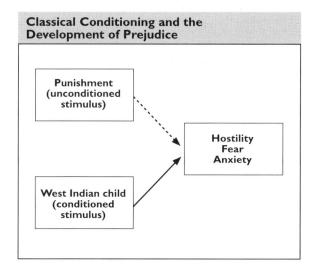

Classical Conditioning and the Development of Prejudice

Punishment (unconditioned stimulus) ⤍ Hostility Fear Anxiety

West Indian child (conditioned stimulus) → Hostility Fear Anxiety

Moreover, these individuals are usually highly conventional and cynical.

Much of the recent research on right-wing authoritarianism (RWA) has been carried out by Altemeyer (1981, 1988) who has constructed a scale to measure this characteristic. Some of the items from his RWA scale are:

The way things are going in this country, it's going to take a lot of "strong medicine" to straighten out the troublemakers, criminals, and perverts.

It would be best for everyone if the proper authorities censored magazines and movies to keep trashy material away from the youths.

The real keys to the "good life" are obedience, discipline, and sticking to the straight and narrow.

An authoritarian would agree with the items above and disagree with items such as:

There is nothing wrong with premarital intercourse.

"Free speech" means that people should even be allowed to make speeches and write books urging the overthrow of the government.

There is absolutely nothing wrong with nudist camps.

In addition to confirming that authoritarians are conventional, highly submissive to authority, and aggressive toward those they believe to be inferior or "different," Altemeyer (1988) found that they also are self-righteous and feel themselves to be morally superior. Esses, Haddock and Zanna (1993) report that English Canadians who were identified as high authoritarians by Altemeyer's scale had more negative attitudes toward four minority groups (French Canadians, Native Indians, Pakistanis and homosexuals) than low authoritarians. This was especially evident in their judgement of Pakistanis and homosexuals.

One other manifestation of authoritarian aggression may be *scapegoating*. Scapegoating may occur when individuals are frustrated by conditions or situations they cannot directly control or change, e.g., "the economic situation" or "the government." When the source of the frustration is vague and difficult to locate, tension and hostility may be aroused and *displaced* onto a convenient out-group. This out-group is then blamed for the discomfort and difficulties being experienced. Much of the treatment of the Jews during the Nazi regime in Germany may have been an example of scapegoating. Jews were blamed for all the economic woes that the Germans experienced after World War I and into the 1930s. A more recent example may be the frequently heard claim that immigrants are taking jobs away from Canadians.

The proportion of individuals who can be described as extreme authoritarians is not large but is often compensated by their vociferousness. Among them may be found individuals who belong to neo-Nazi and white-supremacist movements, distribute hate literature, publish newsletters warning us that psychiatry is a Communist plot, insist that J.D. Salinger's *Catcher in the Rye* or Margaret Laurence's *The Diviners* be removed from school curricula and libraries, or (as happened in Manitoba) have teachers fired who suggest that their students read unconventional newspapers like the *Georgia Straight*. In some instances, the concerns of such individuals border on the ludicrous. For example, a women's association in Texas demanded that *Robin Hood* be removed from the local library because it glorified Communism. (He took from the rich and gave to the poor.) In 1981, the trustees of a school district in Ontario removed John Steinbeck's *The Grapes of Wrath* from high school classrooms to review it for its "suitability." (The Nobel prize winner was in good company, however. Among other works removed during the purge were *The Apprenticeship of Duddy Kravitz* by Mordecai Richler, *Sons and Lovers* by D.H. Lawrence, and *Waiting for Godot* by Samuel Beckett.)

An additional serious social consequence of the authoritarian personality has been suggested by Bray and Noble (1978). They discovered, in a mock-jury experiment, that high authoritarians reached guilty verdicts more frequently and imposed more severe punishments than low authoritarians.

Parents, for better or worse, eventually give up their role as the major influence in children's lives. As children grow older their world increases in size. They begin to interact with peers, enter school, begin to read and spend some of each day watching TV. All of these situations may contribute to the formation or reinforcement of prejudice.

Teachers and schools

While parents are the child's first authority figures, other people—teachers, for instance—also exert considerable influence. Like everyone else, teachers have their prejudices and, although they may try to be as tolerant as possible, there are many opportunities in the classroom for less-than-desirable attitudes to be communicated to the pupils. For example, how will children in multiracial classrooms be treated? How will children who are either the butt or the source of racial slurs be handled? Certain courses, such as geography and history, give the teacher the opportunity to impart *correct* information about ethnic, racial, or other groups—but there are dangers here as well. Does the teacher give equal time to both sides of an issue? Can attitudes toward Communism be held in check during a discussion about recent Russian or Chinese history? And, if not all topics can be covered in the time allotted, how is a decision made about what material should be omitted?

Until recently, when some of the worst examples started to be eliminated, many textbooks contained biased and inaccurate information about ethnic and other groups. For example, the Canadian Indian was frequently depicted as an alcohol-addicted, primitive savage with only a rudimentary social organization (conversely, the depiction was highly sentimental). Texts also typically relegated males and females to traditional roles. (In some cases, modifications of texts and other books designed to correct these biases have been overzealous, creating some backlash. Activist journalist June Callwood (1987) recently castigated the Canadian publishing industry for producing "sanitized" books reflecting a "pious" history that never was.) Bias has also been evident in the *context* in which material is presented to the student. For instance, how is the student affected when his or her arithmetic problems involve only white collar business applications? Why is it that union officials or plumbers never do any calculations? The context within which problems are set can convey to students the attitudes and values of the instructor or text author.

The media

Textbooks are only a step away from the mass media: magazines, newspapers, radio, television, and films. North American children spend a lot of time watching TV. In fact Lambert and Klineberg (1967) have reported that by the age of ten, children obtain most of their information from TV and school rather than from their parents. There are numerous ways in which attitudes can be influenced by the media—through selective or biased reporting in newspapers or by the repetition of stereotypes in television shows.

Visible minorities rarely appear in television commercials or magazine advertising in Canada. A survey conducted in Canada by Lateef and Bangash (1977) found that television commercials observed over a four-day period involved 2064 persons of whom only 48 were visible minority members. If the commercials of charitable organizations (e.g., CARE) and those from the United States are omitted, the percentage of visible minority members drops to .09 percent of the total commercials on television.

Six years later, in 1983, Moore and Cadeau (1985) analyzed the content of 1733 Canadian television commercials. They found that 88 percent of the voice-overs were done by men, fewer than two percent of the commercials included elderly people as central characters and, if elderly people were involved, they were most likely to be men. Visible minorities appeared in fewer than four percent of all commercials. Moreover, Aranoff (1974) has reported that when the elderly appear in television programs, they are portrayed more negatively than other age groups.

One television series, *All in the Family*, popular in the '70s, stimulated considerable discussion. Some people argued that by allowing the major character, Archie Bunker, to express his bigoted views, similar views held by audience members would be strengthened (Brigham and Giesbrecht, 1976). A research study conducted by Vidmar and Rokeach (1974) provides a tentative response to this issue. They theorized that (1) viewers would get out of the program what they expect to get (*selective perception*); and (2) bigots and non-bigots would differ in the frequency with which they watch the show (*selective exposure*). The subjects in this experiment, Canadian adults and American adolescents, were first administered an attitude scale and then divided into two groups, "prejudiced" and "non-prejudiced." Next their reactions to *All in the Family* were compared. The major findings revealed that those in the prejudiced group liked bigoted Archie more than his liberal son-in-law, Mike, and that they admired Archie's values. However, the two groups did not differ in their overall enjoyment of the show. The experiment also indicated that those who watched the program more often also were likely to score higher on the measure of prejudice. It is important to note that the overall frequency of television viewing in general was not higher among the prejudiced than the non-prejudiced group, suggesting that the prejudiced were more attracted to this particular program. Pending further evidence, we can conclude that such programs may increase or strengthen prejudice depending on the predispositions of the viewers. That Canadians might not respond in the same way as Americans was found in another study

(Surlin and Tate, 1976) which showed that Americans in Athens, Georgia, thought the *All in the Family* episodes were more humorous than did viewers in Saskatoon.

Peer groups

Peers exercise more influence over attitudes as the child matures. By adolescence, peers are likely to be more influential in many respects than a child's parents. In the early years, parents exercise considerable control over children's relationships and, since playmates are likely to come from similar socioeconomic backgrounds, attitudes encountered in the home are likely to be reinforced and strengthened outside of it. But as children grow older, their contacts become more diverse and they are less apt to be influenced by parental standards. Like parents, the members of peer groups are effective in influencing attitudes and behaviour because they offer information, reward conformity, and punish non-conformity. This pressure to conform, which continues throughout a person's life, is powerful and hard to resist. Thus, expressing ideas and beliefs which the group considers to be correct is just as important as wearing clothes which the group considers to be appropriate. Indeed, Pettigrew (1961) argues that in the United States most prejudice is based on conformity. One welcome aspect of this theory is that unlike prejudice associated with deep-seated personality patterns, prejudice based on conformity may be more flexible. If the group norm changes or if individuals join new groups with different views, then their attitudes will likely shift in the same direction.

A Textbook of Social Psychology, Third Edition, J. E. Alcock, D. W. Carment, S. W. Sadava, © 1994. Used by permission of Prentice Hall Canada Inc.

TASK

Listening for Solutions

● GUIDED NOTETAKING

INTERGROUP CONTACT AND REDUCING PREJUDICE

Listen to the information carefully, filling in the outline below with point-form notes.

After you have finished, compare your notes with those of a partner and then discuss the lecture with the class.

Intergroup Contact

DEFINITION:

Three conditions to be met:

1.

2.

3.

Three other factors needing consideration:

1.

2.

3.

Public Awareness Campaign

Based on your understanding of the issues discussed in this unit, you will create a campaign for fighting prejudice and raising awareness of Canada's multicultural heritage and race relations issues. Work with a partner.

1. Prepare a written plan for implementing this public awareness campaign. Your plan should include the following:

   a) A **rationale** for the campaign. This section of your plan should discuss the issues surrounding race relations and provide an outline of the problems your campaign will address. Explain the need for such a campaign.

   b) A profile of the **audience** for the campaign. Who needs to hear this message? Where can they be reached?

   c) A description of the **content** of the campaign. What information will you include? What questions will you raise? How?

   d) A **media** outline for the campaign. What media will you use to create public awareness of these issues? You should try to include **three** of the following types of media messages:

video mini-documentary	*audio advertisement*
billboard	*video advertisement*
poster	*in-school program*
print advertisement	*workplace program*

2. Before you start, survey existing public awareness campaigns on impaired driving, AIDS awareness, and other social issues.

3. Create the three media messages that you have chosen.

4. Hold an exhibition when all class members have completed their campaigns. Invite other classes or the public at large to share the messages you have created, and to evaluate the impact and effectiveness of your work.

Part A: 20 Qs – 10 marks

B: 3 – 4 you do 1 • 1~5 marks
                        +

C: 3 – 4 you do 1 1~5 Marks.
                +
                20 marks.

Court and Criminal trial.